# "Thus Sayeth the Lord"

## Beyond Biblical Exegesis: Revelation by the Most Honorable Elijah Muhammad

# "Thus Sayeth the Lord"

## Beyond Biblical Exegesis: Revelation by the Most Honorable Elijah Muhammad

---

Compiled by Mecca and Michael Muhammad

**A-Team Publishing**

Atlanta, Georgia

# "Thus Sayeth the Lord"

## Beyond Biblical Exegesis: Revelation by the Most Honorable Elijah Muhammad

February 2010

Copyright © 2010, Our Book Publishing

*All rights reserved. No part of this book may be reproduced or transmitted in any form or by any means without written permission from the publisher except in the case of reviews and articles.*

## Table of Contents

**Preface** ................................................................ 9

**Introduction** ..................................................... 11

**Chapter 1** (Genesis) ......................................... 15

**Chapter 2** (Exodus) .......................................... 37

**Chapter 3** (Leviticus) ........................................ 48

**Chapter 4** (Numbers) ....................................... 51

**Chapter 5** (Deuteronomy) ................................ 54

**Chapter 6** (I Kings) ........................................... 58

**Chapter 7** (I Chronicles) ................................... 60

**Chapter 8** (II Chronicles) .................................. 62

**Chapter 9** (Job) ................................................. 65

**Chapter 10** (Psalms) .......................................... 65

**Chapter 11** (Proverbs) ....................................... 75

**Chapter 12** (Isaiah) ............................................ 78

**Chapter 14** (Jeremiah) ..................................... 106

**Chapter 15** (Ezekiel) ........................................ 118

**Chapter 16** (Daniel) ......................................... 125

**Chapter 17** (Hosea) ......................................... 130

*Table of Contents*

**Chapter 18** (Joel) .................................. 131

**Chapter 19** (Obadiah) ......................... 135

**Chapter 20** (Jonah) ............................. 136

**Chapter 21** (Nahum) ........................... 137

**Chapter 22** (Habakkuk) ...................... 139

**Chapter 23** (Zechariah) ...................... 144

**Chapter 24** (Malachi) ......................... 145

**Chapter 25** (Matthew) ........................ 147

**Chapter 26** (Mark) .............................. 161

**Chapter 27** (Luke) .............................. 166

**Chapter 28** (John) ............................... 178

**Chapter 29** (I John) ............................ 190

**Chapter 30** (I Corinthians) ................. 191

**Chapter 31** (II Corinthians) ............... 194

**Chapter 32** (II Thessalonians) ........... 195

**Chapter 33** (James) ............................. 199

**Chapter 34** (I Peter) ........................... 202

**Chapter 35** (II Peter) .......................... 203

**Chapter 36** (Revelation) ..................... 205

## Dedication

This compilation is dedicated to the Most Honorable Elijah Muhammad, The Honorable Minister Louis Farrakhan and the Lost Found Nation of Islam in the West.

**The Saviour, Master W. Fard Muhammad**

"The knowledge of Allah, the Supreme Being, and the true religion (Islam) had never been taught to us by anyone before the coming of Allah in the Person of Master Fard Muhammad."

**The Most Hon. Elijah Muhammad**

# Preface

This work is compiled with great humility and respect for the Most Honorable Elijah Muhammad, the Honorable Minister Louis Farrakhan and the Nation of Islam. The wisdom of the Most Honorable Elijah Muhammad will forever resonate in the hearts and minds of the human family for generations to come. The continued work of the Honorable Minister Louis Farrakhan is a testimony of the success of the teachings of the Honorable Elijah Muhammad. Through careful study and investigation of the many truths of the Bible, we learn to see prophesies and our present condition, the enemy of God, and the divinity of the Hon. Elijah Muhammad in his exalted state as **Messiah**. There are many falsehoods that will trap the ignorant and prudent reader. However, with a sincere disposition and constant study of the words of the Honorable Elijah Muhammad, students of the Bible will learn and mature in his wisdom, that they may become wise and speak the *revealed* word of Allah (Master Fard Muhammad) as he taught it to his servant.

Divine guidance comes from observance of the Divine one who is the Guide. The Honorable Minister Louis Farrakhan is divinely guided. Minister Farrakhan's deep devotion, love and perfect approach to God's wisdom and his consistent WORK, obedience, and commitment to the Honorable Elijah Muhammad's mission; invokes faith in the faithless who desire a redeemer. Thus, the task of raising a mentally and spiritually dead people cannot be accomplished through the Bible, with mere seminary taught exegesis. The objective of this compilation is to help us feed on the words of the Honorable Elijah

Muhammad in this dark hour, that we may see the Light of Allah's Glory.

> As we near the exhaustion of the Wisdom of this world which has not been able to shed enough light on our path in search for that Supreme Wisdom to keep us from stumbling and falling, we now seek the wisdom of Allah, the Best Knower and Guide in the Person of Master Fard Muhammad (to Whom be praised forever). The reader will find that light in this book.

These are words of the Most Hon. Elijah Muhammad, taken from the Preface of *Message to the Blackman in America*. The reader will find that light in the Honorable Elijah Muhammad's words compiled in this book.

Michael T. Muhammad - February 21, 2010

# Introduction

...because my people do not know any Scripture or ever read any Scripture other than the Bible (which they do not understand), I thought it best to make them understand the book which they read and believe in, since the Bible is their graveyard and they must be awakened from it. There are many Muslims who do not care to read anything in the Bible. But those Muslims have not been given my job.

The Most Honorable Elijah Muhammad
*Message to the Blackman in America*

Exegesis is defined by Michael J. Gorman, in his book *Elements of Biblical Exegesis: A basic guide for Students and Ministers:*

> ...as the careful historical, literary, and the theological analysis of a text. ... "scholarly reading", ... reading in the way that "ascertains" the sense of the text in the most complete, systematic recording possible of the phenomena of the text and grappling with the reasons that speak for or against a specific understanding of it. Another appropriate description of exegesis is "close reading" a term borrowed from the study of literature. "Close" reading means the deliberate, word-by-word and phrase-by-phrase consideration of all the parts of a text in order to understand it as a whole. Those who engage in the process of exegesis are called exegetes.[1]

From a cursory glance of Gorman's words, some may think his definition describes what the Honorable Elijah

---

[1] Michael J. Gorman, *Elements of Biblical Exegesis.* (Peabody, MA: Hendrickson, 2001) 8-9.

Muhammad said and taught about the Bible. I would disagree. Gorman's definition of the word *exegesis* does not appropriately define the Most Honorable Elijah Muhammad's wisdom of the scriptures, nor does it provide insight into the process or methodology that Master Fard Muhammad used to teach the Hon. Elijah Muhammad. His definition may very well define the process and practices of a seminary student, but not a student taught directly by God.

Thus, the sub-title of this book is appropriately called, *"Beyond Biblical Exegesis, Divine Revelation by the Most Honorable Elijah Muhammad"*. Exegesis is considered a *conversation* [2] with the text and those historical figures living and dead that contributed to the text. It is considered the process of critical analysis and investigation of the text, i.e., the Bible. What is it called when a person has a conversation with God? What if he is taught by God? By what process does understanding HIS words in the Bible involve? Is it exegesis?

The Hon. Elijah Muhammad is not an exegete. There has never been a man to be taught by God in America, except the Hon. Elijah Muhammad. [3] The direct word of God, from his mouth, goes beyond contemporary exegetical thought, scriptural criticism and interpretation. The Hon. Elijah Muhammad affirms the Godhood of this Supreme *God* in his book "Our Saviour Has Arrived":

> Allah is all of us. But we have a Supreme One that we can throw this name "Holy" upon. He is Allah, The One over all of us; The Most Supreme One, the Wisest

---

[2] **Elements of Biblical Exegesis**, 10.

[3] Jabril Muhammad, *This is the One: The Honored Elijah Muhammad, We need not look for another*, 3rd ed. (USA. 1996) 17.

One, the Mightiest One; The One that Sees and Hears that which we can't see and hear. That Is He. He is rooted in all of us. Every righteous person is a god. We are all God. When we say "Allah" we mean every righteous person. Allah teaches me that He is a man.[4]

This **Allah**, Mr. Muhammad says appeared as a man who taught him for a period of time equal to three years and half years:

> According to the teachings to me of man's histories by Allah (God) in the Person of Master Fard Muhammad, praise is due to Him forever, The Great Mahdi and the Messiah that the world has been expected to come for the last two thousand years, has come and is going about His work as has been predicted that He would do. He taught me for three years (night and day) on the histories of the two people, Black and white. What he taught me verifies the teachings of the Bible and Holy Qur'an (if rightly understood) of the two people, Black and white. He said that there was no birth record of the Black Man and therefore none can say how old the Black Nation is. As far back as, He said, a record has been kept, it dates 76 trillion years. These years (76 trillion) were divided into periods of six trillion years beyond 66 trillion years which make the said figure 76 would be 78, instead of 76 trillion.[5]

It is this wisdom mentioned above, which is *beyond exegesis*, and is in fact *Divine Revelation*. Maulana Muhammad Ali in his book ***The Religion of Islam*** explains the highest form of revelation as a spoken word:

---

[4] Elijah Muhammad, *Our Saviour Has Arrived*. (Chicago, IL: Muhammad Temple No. 2, 1974) 26.
[5] Ibid, 96-97.

> For the delivery of the higher message which relates to the welfare of mankind, a higher form of revelation is chosen, a form in which the message is not simply an idea but is clothed in actual words. The Prophet's faculty of being spoken to by God is so highly developed that he receives the messages, not only as ideas instilled into the mind or in the form of words uttered or heard under influence of the Holy Spirit, but actually as Divine messages in words delivered through the latter.[6]

Ali in his explanation of *revelation* suggests that in its higher form, it is "clothed in actual words", as it is received when "being spoken to by God". The other two forms of revelation come in forms that are lesser, yet still divine in their manner.[7] According to Ali's interpretation of what the Holy Quran describes as *revelation*; we cannot call exegesis. This is certainly a subject worthy of attention in a public discourse. It is the firm truth that the Honorable Elijah Muhammad was indeed taught by Almighty Allah who appeared in the person of Master W.F. Muhammad. He taught the Honorable Elijah Muhammad, the words that have been compiled in this small book.

Michael T. Muhammad
February 21, 2010

---

[6] Maulana M. Ali, *The Religion of Islam*. (Columbus, OH: Ahmadiyya Anjuman Isha'at Islam, 1990), 17-19.
[7] On the two lower forms of revelation see Ali, **Religion of Islam**, 17-19.

# Chapter I:

## The Old Testament

## Genesis

The first phrase in the Hebrew text of 1:1 is *bereshith* ("in [the] beginning"), which is also the Hebrew title of the book (books in ancient times customarily were named after their first word or two). The English title, Genesis, is Greek in origin and comes from the word *geneseos*, which appears in the pre-Christian Greek translation (Septuagint) of 2:4; 5:1. Depending on its context, the word can mean "birth," "genealogy," or "history of origin." In both its Hebrew and Greek forms, then, the traditional title of Genesis appropriately describes its contents, since it is primarily a book of beginnings.[8]

**Genesis 1:1 King James Version (KJV)-** In the beginning God created the Heaven and Earth.

**Genesis 1:1 New International Version (NIV)-** In the beginning God created the heavens and the earth.

> **Honorable Elijah Muhammad (HEM)-** From the first day that the white race received the Divine Scripture they started tampering with its truth to make it suit themselves, and blind the black man. It is their nature to do evil, and the Book can't be recognized as the pure and Holy Word of God. It opens with the words of

---

[8] Ronald Youngblood, *Introduction: Genesis*, in *New International Version Study Bible* (Grand Rapids, MI: Zondervan, 2002), 1.

someone other than God trying to represent God and His Creation to us. This is called the Book of Moses and reads as follows: *In the beginning God created Heaven and Earth* (Gen. 1:1). When was this beginning? There in the Genesis the writer tells us that it was 4,004 B.C. This we know, now, that it refers to the making of the white race and not the heavens and earth.[9]

> **HEM-** The above is said by representatives of God and not directly from the mouth of God although the words are true. The whole of the book called Genesis of the Bible is said to be Moses' Book and what Moses' said of the history of God's creation; and of Adam, Seth, Enos, Methuselah, Lamech, Noah, Abraham, Lot and Melchizedek. Now God has not addressed Himself to us in Genesis, the opening of the Bible; it is His Prophet, Moses.[10]

**Genesis 1:2 KJV-** And the earth was without form and void; darkness was upon the deep and the spirit of God moved upon the face of the waters.

**Genesis 1:2 NIV-** Now the earth was formless and empty, darkness was over the surface of the deep, and the Spirit of God was hovering over the waters.

> **HEM-** The second verse of the first chapter of Genesis reads: And the earth was without form and void; darkness was upon the deep and the spirit of God moved upon the face of the waters. What was the

---

[9] Elijah Muhammad, *Message to the Blackman in America*.(Chicago, IL: Muhammad Temple No.2, 1965) 94-95.
[10] Muhammad, *Our Saviour Has Arrived*. 63.

water on, since there was no form of earth? As I see it, the Bible is very questionable.[11]

**Genesis 1:1-31 KJV-** In the beginning God created the heaven and the earth. And the earth was without form, and void; and darkness was upon the face of the deep. And the Spirit of God moved upon the face of the waters. And God said, Let there be light: and there was light. And God saw the light, that it was good: and God divided the light from the darkness. And God called the light Day, and the darkness he called Night. And the evening and the morning were the first day. And God said, Let there be a firmament in the midst of the waters, and let it divide the waters from the waters. And God made the firmament, and divided the waters which were under the firmament from the waters which were above the firmament: and it was so. And God called the firmament Heaven. And the evening and the morning were the second day. And God said, Let the waters under the heaven be gathered together unto one place, and let the dry land appear: and it was so. And God called the dry land Earth; and the gathering together of the waters called the Seas: and God saw that it was good.[12]

**Genesis 1:1-31 NIV-** In the beginning God created the heavens and the earth. Now the earth was formless and empty, darkness was over the surface of the deep, and the Spirit of God was hovering over the waters. And God

---

[11] Muhammad, *Message to the Blackman*, 95.

[12] Genesis 1:1-10 appears here, but it is recommended that the reader review the entire reading up Gen. 1:31 as referenced by the Most Honorable Elijah Muhammad.

said, "Let there be light," and there was light. God saw that the light was good, and He separated the light from the darkness. God called the light "day," and the darkness he called "night." And there was evening, and there was morning the first day. And God said, "Let there be an expanse between the waters to separate water from water." So God made the expanse and separated the water under the expanse from the water above it. And it was so. God called the expanse "sky." And there was evening, and there was morning—the second day. And God said, "Let the water under the sky be gathered to one place, and let dry ground appear." And it was so. God called the dry ground "land," and the gathered waters he called "seas." And God saw that it was good.[13]

> **HEM-** There His creation is pointed out to us as a proof that there is a Supreme Being over all this universe and that it was made in six days (Genesis 1:1-31) God does not address Himself to us throughout the first chapter. Not His religion or even the name of the representation of God is mentioned there. This reader is without authentic proof of just who is the author of the book called Genesis. You must remember that from the King James authorized version of the Bible, it has been only 346 years and you have only been permitted to read the Bible for the past 90 years. The white man, our slave master and enemy had the Bible over 250 years before we were allowed to read the book.[14]

**Genesis 1:26 KJV-** And God said, Let us make man in our image, after our likeness: and let them have dominion over

---

[13] See footnote 4.

[14] Muhammad, *Our Saviour Has Arrived*, 155-156.

the fish of the sea, and over the fowl of the air, and over the cattle, and over all the earth, and over every creeping thing that creepeth upon the earth.

**Genesis 1:26 NIV-** Then God said, "Let us make man in our image, in our likeness, and let them rule over the fish of the sea and the birds of the air, over the livestock, over all the earth, and over all the creatures that move along the ground."

> **HEM-** In the Bible, referring to their creation, we have US (Gen. 1:26) creating, or rather making the race; the US and WE used show beyond a shadow of a doubt that they came from another people. Knowledge of the white race removes once and for all times the mistakes that would be made in dealing with them. My followers and I can and are getting along with them in a more understandable way than ever because we know them. You cannot blame one for the way he or she was born, for they had nothing to do with that. Can we say to them why don't you do the righteousness when nature did not give righteousness to them? Or say to them, why are you such a wicked devil? Who is responsible, the made or the maker? Yet we are not excused for following and practicing his evil or accepting him for a righteous guide just because he is not his maker.[15]

> **HEM-** After God had created everything without asking anyone for help, then comes His weakness in the 26th verse of the same chapter (Gen. 1:26). He invites us to help Him make a man. Allah has revealed the "US" that was invited to make a man (white race).

---

[15] Muhammad, *Message to the Blackman*, 54.

A man is far easier to make than the heavens and earth. We can't charge these questionable readings of the Bible to Musa because he was a prophet of God, and they don't lie.[16]

**HEM-** Again, we learn who the Bible (Genesis 1:26) is referring to in the saying: Let us make man. This US was fifty-nine thousand, nine hundred and ninety-nine (59,999) black men and women; making or grafting them into the likeness or image of the original man. Now that they are the same, but have the ways of a human being they are referred to as mankind -- not the real original man, but a being made like the original in the sense of human beings.[17]

**HEM-** The above was all necessary if the devils were to rule as a God of the world. They must conquer, and bring into subjection, all life upon the earth -- not land life alone, but they must subdue the sea and the like therein -- master everything, until a greater master of God comes, which would mean the end of their power over the life of our earth.

We all bear witness that the scripture quoted above refers to the Caucasian race. They are the only people who answer that description and word for the past 4,000 years. They have subdued the people and most every kind of living thing upon the earth. God has blessed them to exercise all their knowledge, and blessed them with guides (prophets) from among our own people; and, with the rain and seasons of the earth. Today, their wealth is great upon the earth. Their sciences of worldly goods have sent them, not only after the wealth of other than their own people,

---

[16] Muhammad, *Message to the Blackman*, 95.
[17] Ibid., 118.

but even after the lives and property of their own kind. They have tried to re-people (replenish) the earth with their own kind, by skillfully killing off the black man and mixing their blood into the black woman.[18]

**Genesis 1:27 KJV-** So God created man in his own image, in the image of God created he him; male and female created he them.

**Genesis 1:27 NIV-** So God created man in his own image, in the image of God he created him; male and female he created them.

> **HEM-** God created them in His image (Gen. 1:27). They are in the image and likeness of a human being (black man), but are altogether different kind of human being than that of the black human beings. Their pale white skin; their blue eyes (even disliked by themselves) tells any black man or woman, that in those blue and green eyes, there just can't be any sincere love and friendship for them. They are unlike and we are like. Like repels -- unlike attracts. The very characteristics of black and white are so very different.[19]

> **HEM-** We know that God exists and is All Wise, All Powerful, and that this quickening power called spirit is from Him. But who is this God? A spirit cannot think, but thinking can produce spirit. So according to God's own words, through His prophets, He must be a man. He is interested in man's affairs according to the Bible (Genesis 1:27): "God created man in His own

---

[18] Muhammad, *Message to the Blackman*, 121. See also II Thess. 2:9.
[19] Ibid.

image and likeness, both male and female." If we believe that alone, that God created man in His own image and likeness that is sufficient for us to expect God to be nothing other than man.[20]

**Genesis 1:29 KJV** - And God said, Behold, I have given you every herb bearing seed, which is upon the face of all the earth, and every tree, in the which is the fruit of a tree yielding seed; to you it shall be for meat.

**Genesis 1:29 NIV** - Then God said, "I give you every seed-bearing plant on the face of the whole earth and every tree that has fruit with seed in it. They will be yours for food."

> **HEM-** We do not need to eat everything just because the Bible (in Genesis) said that Adam (who represents the white race) could eat nearly all of the herbs of the earth (that are not poisonous). Our scientists teach us of that which is not poisonous. [21]

> **HEM-** And I would not like you to follow the Bible in Genesis, where Adam is told to go and eat of all the herbs of the earth. There are some poisonous herbs that would have killed Adam. This is a mistake that the theologians put in the Bible. You cannot eat all the herbs; some of them will kill you. But, eat the best of herbs that God approves for you and me and do not think He approved of Adam eating all the herbs of the earth.[22]

---

[20] Muhammad, *Our Saviour Has Arrived*, 66.
[21] Muhammad, *How to Eat to Live, Book One*, 3.
[22] Ibid., 104.

> The Bible has a very ignorant way of teaching us the proper foods. In the beginning of the creation of Adam, in Genesis it says, every herb and all the fruits of the trees are good for you to eat. It is ignorant to believe such a thing as that. You try it (eating all of these things) and you will die.[23]

**Genesis 2:17- KJV** But of the tree of the knowledge of good and evil, thou shalt not eat of it: for in the day that thou eatest thereof thou shalt surely die.

**Genesis 2:17 NIV-** But you must not eat from the tree of the knowledge of good and evil, for when you eat of it you will surely die.

> **HEM-** The Bible's forbidden tree was a tree of the knowledge of good and evil. This also tells us that the tree was a person, for trees know nothing! This tree of knowledge was forbidden to Adam & Eve. The only one whom this tree could be is the devil. After deceiving Adam and his wife, he has been called a serpent due to his keen knowledge of tricks and his acts of shrewdness; he made his acquaintance with Adam and his wife in the absence of God. Since this is the nature of a liar, he can best lie to the people when truth is absent.[24]

> **HEM-** Adam and Eve (the father and mother of the white race (Yakub is the real name) refused the religion of Islam (peace) because of the nature in which they were made. This makes it impossible for the white race to submit to Allah and obey His law of righteousness.

---

[23] Muhammad, *How to Eat to Live, Book Two*, 81.

[24] Muhammad, *Message to the Blackman*, 126-127.

This, the lost-found members of the Asiatic nation from the Tribe of Shabazz must learn of the white race: that it is a waste of time to seek mercy and justice from a people who by nature do not have it for each other. They talk and preach the goodness of God and His prophets only to deceive you, who by nature are of the God of Righteousness, into following them away from our God to a god who does not exist.[25]

**Genesis 3:1 KJV-** Now the serpent was more subtle than any beast of the field which the LORD God had made. And he said unto the woman, Yea, hath God said, Ye shall not eat of every tree of the garden?

**Genesis 3:1 NIV -** Now the serpent was more crafty than any of the wild animals the LORD God had made. He said to the woman, "Did God really say, 'You must not eat from any tree in the garden'?"

> **HEM-** In Gen (3:1) he appeared in the garden of Paradise before the woman who was ready to be delivered to devour her child as soon as it is born. The serpent, the devil, dragon, Satan, seems to have been seeking the weaker part of man (the woman) to bring to naught the man- the Divine Man. It is his first and last trick to deceive the people of God through the woman or with the woman. He is using his woman to tempt the black man by parading her half-nude before his eyes and with public love-making, indecent kissing and dancing over radio and television screens and throughout their public papers and magazines. He is

---

[25] Elijah Muhammad, *The Fall of America*. (Chicago, IL: Muhammad Temple of Islam No.2, 1973) 47.

flooding the world with propaganda against God and His true religion, Islam.[26]

**Genesis 3:6 KJV** - And when the woman saw that the tree was good for food, and that it was pleasant to the eyes, and a tree to be desired to make one wise, she took of the fruit thereof, and did eat, and gave also unto her husband with her; and he did eat.

**Genesis 3:6 NIV** - When the woman saw that the fruit of the tree was good for food and pleasing to the eye, and also desirable for gaining wisdom, she took some and ate it. She also gave some to her husband, who was with her, and he ate it.

> **HEM-** Both Jews and Christians are guilty of setting up rivals to Allah (God). Adam and Eve accepted the guidance of the serpent instead of that of Allah (Gen 3:6).[27]

**Genesis 3:13 KJV** - And the LORD God said unto the woman, what is this that thou hast done? And the woman said, the serpent beguiled me, and I did eat.

**Genesis 3:13 NIV** - To Adam he said, "Because you listened to your wife and ate from the tree about which I commanded you, 'You must not eat of it, "Cursed is the ground because of you; through painful toil you will eat of it all the days of your life.

---

[26] Muhammad, *Message to the Blackman*, 127.
[27] Ibid., 74.

> **HEM-** They (Devils) shed the life blood of all life, even their own, and are scientists at deceiving the black people. They deceived the very people of Paradise (3:13). They killed their own brother (4:8). The innocent earth's blood (4:10) revealed to its Maker (the brothers blood cryeth unto me from the ground); The very earth, the soil of America, soaked by this race of devils, now cryeth out to its Maker for her burden of carrying the innocent blood of the righteous slain upon her.[28]

**Genesis 3:15 KJV -** And I will put enmity between thee and the woman, and between thy seed and her seed; it shall bruise thy head, and thou shalt bruise his heel.

**Genesis 3:15 NIV -** And I will put enmity between you and the woman, and between your offspring and hers; he will crush your head, and you will strike his heel.

> **HEM-** This defiant act is against the manifestation of the truth of them. By the Son of Man is the reason He is punishing them. He is putting priest against priest, church against church, and Christians against the Pope of Rome as we see it today Gen. 3:15. The Bible prophesies that the serpent will bruise the heel (followers) of the woman (Messenger). This means they would deceive the followers of the Messenger. But the Messenger will bruise the head of the serpent meaning the foundation of the chief to Christianity's way of teaching.[29]

---

[28] Muhammad, *Message to the Blackman*, 128.

[29] Muhammad, *Our Saviour Has Arrived*, 185.

**Genesis 3: 20-24 KJV -** And Adam called his wife's name Eve; because she was the mother of all living. Unto Adam also and to his wife did the LORD God make coats of skins, and clothed them. And the LORD God said, Behold, the man is become as one of us, to know good and evil: and now, lest he put forth his hand, and take also of the tree of life, and eat, and live forever: Therefore the LORD God sent him forth from the garden of Eden, to till the ground from whence he was taken. So he drove out the man; and he placed at the east of the garden of Eden Cherubims, and a flaming sword which turned every way, to keep the way of the tree of life.

**Genesis 3:20-24 NIV -** Adam named his wife Eve, because she would become the mother of all the living. The LORD God made garments of skin for Adam and his wife and clothed them. And the LORD God said, "The man has now become like one of us, knowing good and evil. He must not be allowed to reach out his hand and take also from the tree of life and eat, and live forever."So the LORD God banished him from the Garden of Eden to work the ground from which he had been taken. After he drove the man out, he placed on the east side of the Garden of Eden cherubim and a flaming sword flashing back and forth to guard the way to the tree of life.

> **HEM-** According to the Bible (Gen. 3:20-24), Adam and his wife were the first parents of all people (white race only) and the first sinners. According to the Word of Allah, he was driven from the Garden of Paradise into the hills and caves of West Asia, or as they now call it, 'Europe,' to live his evil life in the West and not in the Holy Land of the East. 'Therefore, the Lord God sent

him (Adam) forth from the Garden of Eden, to till the ground from whence he was taken.

So He drove out the man; and He placed at the east of the Garden of Eden cherubim's (Muslim guards) and a flaming sword which turned every way to keep the devils out of the way of the tree of life (the Nation of Islam).' The sword of Islam prevented the Adamic race from crossing the border of Europe and Asia to make trouble among the Muslims for 2,000 years after they were driven out of the Holy Land and away from the people, for their mischief-making, lying and disturbing the peace of the righteous nation of Islam.[30]

**Genesis 4:8 KJV** – And Cain talked with Abel his brother: and it came to pass, when they were in the field, that Cain rose up against Abel his brother, and slew him.

**Genesis 4:8 NIV** - Now Cain said to his brother Abel, "Let's go out to the field." And while they were in the field, Cain attacked his brother Abel and killed him.

**Genesis 4:10 KJV** - And he said, What hast thou done? The voice of thy brother's blood crieth unto me from the ground.

**Genesis 4:10 NIV** - The LORD said, "What have you done? Listen! Your brother's blood cries out to me from the ground.

> **HEM-** According to the word of Allah (God) and the history of the world, since the grafting of the Caucasian race 6,000 years ago, they have caused more

---

[30] Muhammad, *Message to the Blackman*, 133.

bloodshed than any people known to the black nation. Born murderers, their very nature is to murder. The Bible and Holy Quran-an Sharrieff are full of teachings of this bloody race of devils. They shed the life blood of all life, even their own, and are scientists at deceiving the black people. They deceived the very people of Paradise (Bible, Gen. 3:13). They killed their own brother (Gen. 4:8). The innocent earth's blood (Gen. 4:10) revealed it to its Maker (thy brother's blood cryeth unto me from the ground). The very earth, the soil of America, soaked with the innocent blood of the so-called Negroes shed by this race of devils, now crieth out to its Maker for her burden of carrying the innocent blood of the righteous slain upon her.[31]

**Genesis 5:24 KJV -** And Enoch walked with God: and he was not; for God took him.

**Genesis 5:24 NIV -** Enoch walked with God; then he was no more, because God took him away.

**Genesis 6:3 KJV -** And the LORD said, my spirit shall not always strive with man, for that he also is flesh: yet his days shall be an hundred and twenty years.

**Genesis 6:3 NIV -** Then the LORD said, "My Spirit will not contend with man forever, for he is mortal; his days will be a hundred and twenty years."

**Genesis 6:13 KJV -** And God said unto Noah, The end of all flesh is come before me; for the earth is filled with

---

[31] Muhammad, *Message to the Blackman*, 128.

violence through them; and, behold, I will destroy them with the earth.

**Genesis 6:13 NIV** - So God said to Noah, "I am going to put an end to all people, for the earth is filled with violence because of them. I am surely going to destroy both them and the earth."

> **HEM-** Let us check on the Bible and Holy Qur'an and see whether or not we should see a spirit or see a man for God... The Bible says 'Enoch walked with God (Genesis 5:24). 'God talked with Noah' (6:13) and to most of the prophets. Can He be a man or other than a man? God said that 'His spirit shall not always strive with man for that he also is flesh (Genesis 6:3). We have a great subject before us to open up to the world. So have patience and, by the help of Allah, I shall prove to you that God is man.[32]

**Genesis 9:21-25 KJV** - And he drank of the wine, and was drunken; and he was uncovered within his tent. And Ham, the father of Canaan, saw the nakedness of his father, and told his two brethren without. And Shem and Japheth took a garment, and laid it upon both their shoulders, and went backward, and covered the nakedness of their father; and their faces were backward, and they saw not their father's nakedness. And Noah awoke from his wine, and knew what his younger son had done unto him. And he said, Cursed be Canaan; a servant of servants shall he be unto his brethren.

---

[32] Muhammad, *Our Saviour Has Arrived*, 64; Genesis 5:24;6:3; and 6:13 are mentioned in this quote wherein the Most Honorable Elijah Muhammad makes reference to God being a Man.

**Genesis 9:21-25 NIV** -When he drank some of its wine, he became drunk and lay uncovered inside his tent. Ham, the father of Canaan, saw his father's nakedness and told his two brothers outside. But Shem and Japheth took a garment and laid it across their shoulders; then they walked in backward and covered their father's nakedness. Their faces were turned the other way so that they would not see their father's nakedness. When Noah awoke from his wine and found out what his youngest son had done to him, he said, "Cursed be Canaan! The lowest of slaves will he be to his brothers."

> **HEM-** Some believe (in that story of the Bible) that the black people are a curse of Noah on one of his sons (Ham) because this son laughed at his father's nakedness while being drunk from wine (Genesis 9:21-25). The black nation has no birth record. There were as many or more black people on our planet in the days of Noah as there are today. The Bible's record of the flood is 2,348 years before Christ, and if the records are true, we are nearly 4,500 years from Noah's flood. If there were no black people before Noah, then that wicked people who were destroyed in the flood were white people.[33]

**Genesis 9:28, 29 KJV** - "And Noah lived after the flood three hundred and fifty years. And all the days of Noah were nine hundred and fifty years: and he died."

**Genesis 9:28, 29 NIV** - After the flood Noah lived 350 years. Altogether, Noah lived 950 years, and then he died.

---

[33] Muhammad, *Our Saviour Has Arrived*, 87-88.

**HEM-** Allah (God) in the Person of Master Fard Muhammad, to Whom Praises are Due forever, out of His Own Mouth, Said to me that He Causes us to Grow into a New Growth. And that we would have the look and the energy of one who is sixteen (16) years of age and our youth and energy of a sixteen year-old would last forever. In that new life there will be not such things as a stoppage or cease to beget children. As you may read in the Bible Noah was six hundred (600) years old when the flood came (Gen 9:28, 29). That number six hundred (600) is very significant. Noah lived nine hundred and fifty (950) years. The Bible teaches you that he begat children all of those nine hundred and fifty (950) years.[34]

**Genesis 10:10 KJV-** And the beginning of his kingdom was Babel, and Erech, and Accad, and Calneh, in the land of Shinar.

**Genesis 10:10 NIV-** The first centers of his kingdom were Babylon, Erech, Akkad and Calneh, in Shinar.

**HEM-** We say "modern" when we refer to something comparing it to the past. This name "Babylon" begins in Genesis 10:10 (Bible). In Gen. 10:10 it is spelled "B-a-b-e-l." But the same name seems to have changed itself into the name Babylon as we come to the most late-day history of this name. Babel (Babylon) -- According to the history of Babylon throughout the Bible, Babylon is referred to as something prophesied as having a failure upon her progress and rise.[35]

---

[34] Muhammad, *Our Saviour Has Arrived*, 115.
[35] Muhammad, *The Fall of America*, 138.

**Genesis 15:13 KJV-** And he said unto Abram, Know of a surety that thy seed shall be a stranger in a land that is not theirs, and shall serve them; and they shall afflict them four hundred years.

**Genesis 15:13 NIV -** Then the LORD said to him, "Know for certain that your descendants will be strangers in a country not their own, and they will be enslaved and mistreated four hundred years.

> **HEM-** There are many erroneous mistakes made by the scholars and scientists that have caused much misunderstanding of the truth. There are many Arabs throughout the world who cannot bear witness to anyone that another messenger would rise up after Muhammad, who was here nearly 1,400 years ago. This is due to their misunderstanding of the Holy Qur-an and the scriptures of the Prophets Abraham, Moses, Jesus and even Muhammad, himself. They forget that the Bible prophesies of a lost member of the nation of the original people of the earth, who would be lost somewhere on the earth. But neither the Bible nor thee Holy Qur'an specifies the place. The nearest the Bible comes to it is that they would be lost in the wilderness. That fits America.[36]

**Genesis 19:13 KJV-** For we will destroy this place, because the cry of them is waxen great before the face of the LORD; and the LORD hath sent us to destroy it.

---

[36] Muhammad, *Message to the Blackman*, 250.

**Genesis 19:13 NIV-** ...Because we are going to destroy this place. The outcry to the LORD against its people is so great that he has sent us to destroy it.

> **HEM-** The Black woman should be too proud of herself to disgrace herself in the same manner as her white slave-mistress. The Black man should be sent to prison for being such a fool as to allow his wife and daughter to go out and show their nude selves to the public. Nudity originated from the white race. Now they want to say to the world that "I am the guide." The guide to what? The Holy Qur'an says that they lead you to nothing but filth and evil. The Bible is referring to the people of America when it is referring to the people of Sodom and Gomorrah. Allah (God) destroyed them when he saw that it was good to do so. (Gen. 19:13). As it was with Sodom and Gomorrah, so it will be with America.[37]

**Genesis 36:11 KJV-** And the sons of Eliphaz were Teman, Omar, Zepho, and Gatam, and Kenaz.

**Genesis 36:15 KJV -** These were dukes of the sons of Esau: the sons of Eliphaz the firstborn son of Esau; duke Teman, duke Omar, duke Zepho, duke Kenaz.

**Genesis 36:42 KJV -** Duke Kenaz, duke Teman, duke Mibzar.

**Genesis 36:11NIV -** The sons of Eliphaz: Teman, Omar, Zepho, Gatam and Kenaz.

---

[37] Muhammad, *The Fall of America*, 128.

**Genesis 36:15 NIV** - These were the chiefs among Esau's descendants: The sons of Eliphaz the firstborn of Esau:Chiefs Teman, Omar, Zepho, Kenaz.

**Genesis 36:42 NIV** - Kenaz, Teman, Mibzar.

> **HEM-** According to the dictionary of the Bible: Teman, a son of Esau by Adah (Gen. 36:11, 15, 42) and in I Chron. 1:36, now if Habakkuk saw God come or coming from the sons of Esau (Eliphaz), then God must be a man and not a spook.[38]

**Genesis 49:17 KJV-** Dan shall be a serpent by the way, an adder in the path that biteth the horse's heels so that his rider shall fall backward.

**Genesis 49:17 NIV** - Dan will be a serpent by the roadside, a viper along the path, that bites the horse's heels so that its rider tumbles backward.

> **HEM-** Let us refer to Genesis: Dan shall be a serpent by the way, an adder in the path that bitten the horse's heels so that his rider shall fall backward (Gen. 39:17). Here Jacob on his deathbed fourteenth the future of his sons (Moses calls Dan a lion's whelp; he shall leap from Basin; Duet. 33:22). That old serpent, devil and Satan, the old beast, is the dragon which deceiveth the whole world of the poor ignorant darker nations and has caused them to fall off their mount of prosperity, success and independence by accepting advice,

---

[38] Muhammad, *Message to the Blackman*, 7; Muhammad, *Our Saviour Has Arrived*, 68. The explanation for these verses appear in **Message to the Blackman** exactly as they appear in **Our Saviour Has Arrived**. This is the same article printed in both books.

guidance and empty promises which he (the serpent-like Caucasian devil) never intended to fulfill.

How well the prophets have described the characteristics of this race of devils as corresponding to the nature of a snake (serpent). Most snakes wobble and make a crooked trail when and wherever they crawl. So it is with the white race, which goes among the black nation leaving the marks of evil and crooked dealings and doings. In spiritual dealings, there again you will find them like a snake (serpent), following on the heels of the truth bearers (prophets and messengers of God) to bite the believers with false teachings and fear in order that he may cause them to fall off their mount of truth. Like a snake (serpent) he parks in and on the pathway of all the so-called Negroes who seek the way to freedom, truth, justice and equality (Allah and the true religion, Islam).[39]

---

[39] Muhammad, *Message to the Blackman,* 123. Also see 46. Deuteronomy 18:15; Dan is described by Moses as a lions welp.

# Chapter II:

# Exodus

"Exodus" is a Latin word derived from Greek *Exodos*, the name given to the book by those who translated it into Greek. The word means "exit," "departure" (see Lk 9:31; Heb 11:22). The name was retained by the Latin Vulgate, by the Jewish author Philo (a contemporary of Christ) and by the Syriac version. In Hebrew the book is named after its first two words, *we'elleh shemoth* ("These are the names of").

The same phrase occurs in Ge 46:8, where it likewise introduces a list of the names of those Israelites "who went to Egypt with Jacob" (1:1). Thus Exodus was not intended to exist separately, but was thought of as a continuation of a narrative that began in Genesis and was completed in Leviticus, Numbers and Deuteronomy. The first five books of the Bible are together known as the Pentateuch. [40]

**Exodus 3:4 KJV-** And when the LORD saw that he turned aside to see, God called unto him out of the midst of the bush, and said, Moses, Moses. And he said, Here am I.

**Exodus 3:4 NIV -** When the LORD saw that he had gone over to look, God called to him from within the bush, "Moses! Moses!" And Moses said, "Here I am."

**HEM-** The Bible does not claim God to be its author. Jehovah calls to Moses out of the burning bush to go to

---

[40] Walter C. Kaiser and Ronald Youngblood, *Introduction: Exodus*, in *New International Version Study Bible* (Grand Rapids, MI: Zondervan, 2002), 85.

Pharaoh (Ex. 3:9). There is no mention of a book or Bible that is found that Jehovah gave to Moses in the first five books of the Bible, which are claimed to be Moses' books. Moses' rod is the only thing used against Pharaoh and the land of Egypt; and tables of stone in the mountains of Sinai. The miraculous rod of Moses, and not a book, brought Pharaoh and his people to their doom. The Ten Commandments served as a guide for the Jews in the Promised Land. Where do we find in the Bible that it was given to Moses by Jehovah under such name as Bible or the Book?[41]

**Exodus 3:7 KJV** - And the LORD said, I have surely seen the affliction of my people which are in Egypt, and have heard their cry by reason of their taskmasters; for I know their sorrows.

**Exodus 3:7 NIV** - The LORD said, "I have indeed seen the misery of my people in Egypt. I have heard them crying out because of their slave drivers, and I am concerned about their suffering.

> **HEM-** Remember the story of Moses and his people. Jehovah said to Moses: 'I have surely seen the affliction of my people which are in Egypt, and I have heard their cry by reason of their taskmasters; for I know their sorrows' (Ex. 3:7). Jehovah had seen and heard the afflictions and cries of His people while His people were yet dumb to the knowledge of Him, for they called not on Him. They worshipped the gods of Pharaoh and his people. It was to the slaves of Pharaoh and the slaves' fathers that Jehovah, their

---

[41] Muhammad, *Message to the Blackman*, 86.

God, was to show mercy and deliverance. Pharaoh was against Jehovah and His religion and the people who were his slaves. It is time that the mentally dead Negroes, who are afflicted daily by the evil hand of white America, should be delivered and given freedom, justice, and equality and a land that they can call their own. Day and night their cries go up into the ear of Allah, the God of our people (the Muslims).[42]

**Exodus 3:16 KJV -** Go, and gather the elders of Israel together, and say unto them, The LORD God of your fathers, the God of Abraham, of Isaac, and of Jacob, appeared unto me, saying, I have surely visited you, and seen that which is done to you in Egypt.

**Exodus 3:16 NIV -** Go, assemble the elders of Israel and say to them, 'The LORD, the God of your fathers—the God of Abraham, Isaac and Jacob—appeared to me and said: I have watched over you and have seen what has been done to you in Egypt.

> **HEM-** We cannot hope for justice from the devils when by nature there is none in them. All day long the Negroes are mistreated. If Allah and I, His servant, will not stand up for them, who shall stand up for them? You, by far, are unable to do so; for you know not God. The devils have you afraid and worshipping that which you know not. Fear not and come and follow me and God will love you and will set you in heaven at once while you live. Jehovah told Moses to go first to the elders of Israel and say to them: 'The Lord your God (not Pharaoh's) the God of your fathers, He has appeared unto me saying, 'I have

---

[42] Muhammad, *Our Saviour Has Arrived*, 8-9.

surely visited you and have seen that which is done unto you in Egypt (America)' (Exodus 3:16). But the elders would not even meet with Moses, only by way of disputation.[43]

**Exodus 3: 1-4 KJV** - Now Moses kept the flock of Jethro his father in law, the priest of Midian: and he led the flock to the backside of the desert, and came to the mountain of God, even to Horeb. And the angel of the LORD appeared unto him in a flame of fire out of the midst of a bush: and he looked, and, behold, the bush burned with fire, and the bush was not consumed. And Moses said, I will now turn aside, and see this great sight, why the bush is not burnt.

**Exodus 3: 1-4 NIV** - Now Moses was tending the flock of Jethro his father-in-law, the priest of Midian, and he led the flock to the far side of the desert and came to Horeb, the mountain of God. There the angel of the LORD appeared to him in flames of fire from within a bush. Moses saw that though the bush was on fire it did not burn up. So Moses thought, "I will go over and see this strange sight—why the bush does not burn up."

> **HEM-** Jehovah appeared to Moses in the bush. Moses was made to see the bush in a flame of fire though there was no actual fire. The fire represented the anger of Jehovah against Pharaoh and his people. It was a declaration of a divine war against the Egyptians for the deliverance of Israel.[44]

---

[43] Muhammad, *Our Saviour Has Arrived*, 9.
[44] Ibid., 18.

**Exodus 6:3 KJV** - And I appeared unto Abraham, unto Isaac, and unto Jacob, by the name of God Almighty, but by my name JEHOVAH was I not known to them.

**Exodus 6:3 NIV** - I appeared to Abraham, to Isaac and to Jacob as God Almighty, but by my name the LORD I did not make myself known to them.

> **HEM-** The time has arrived that Allah (God) should fulfill His promise made to Abraham. According to the Bible (Gen. 15:13, 14) we do not find wherein Israel had ever sought Jehovah through prayer or from any scripture; nor did they know of any prophet before Moses. The only knowledge we have is in the words of Jehovah's address to Moses- that they knew Him only by the name of God Almighty (Exodus 6:3). But the real issue was not in the name as much as it was in the time. It was the time that Jehovah should fulfill His promise, though Israel was a disbelieving people in Moses and Jehovah.[45]

> **HEM-** They (white people) have nearly all of the poor black preachers on their side to oppose Allah, myself and Islam, the religion of righteous. They will fail and be brought to disgrace as Pharaoh's magicians and he himself were by Allah (God), for you have not known Him, or His religion, as Israel had not known God by His name Jehovah.[46]

**Exodus 16:2-3 KJV** - And the whole congregation of the children of Israel murmured against Moses and Aaron in the wilderness: And the children of Israel said unto them,

---

[45] Muhammad, *Our Saviour Has Arrived*, 18.

[46] Muhammad, *Message to the Blackman*, 21.

Would to God we had died by the hand of the LORD in the land of Egypt, when we sat by the flesh pots, and when we did eat bread to the full; for ye have brought us forth into this wilderness, to kill this whole assembly with hunger.

**Exodus 16:2-3 NIV** - In the desert the whole community grumbled against Moses and Aaron. The Israelites said to them, "If only we had died by the LORD's hand in Egypt! There we sat around pots of meat and ate all the food we wanted, but you have brought us out into this desert to starve this entire assembly to death."

**Exodus 16:8 KJV** - And Moses said, This shall be, when the LORD shall give you in the evening flesh to eat, and in the morning bread to the full; for that the LORD heareth your murmurings which ye murmur against him: and what are we? Your murmurings are not against us, but against the LORD.

**Exodus 16:8 NIV** - Moses also said, "You will know that it was the LORD when he gives you meat to eat in the evening and all the bread you want in the morning, because he has heard your grumbling against him. Who are we? You are not grumbling against us, but against the LORD."

> **HEM-** The Bible shows (Exodus 16:2, 3, 8) that it was the want of bread and meat first of all that gave Moses and Aaron much trouble trying to lead the people into the spiritual knowledge of Jehovah and self-independence. They even said when they were hungry: "Would to God we had died by the hand of

the Lord in the land of Egypt" (Exodus 16:3). Of times, they angered Moses and Aaron by their longing for the food of their slave-masters even while on their way to freedom and self-independence.[47]

**Exodus 16:12-15 KJV** - I have heard the murmurings of the children of Israel: speak unto them, saying, at even ye shall eat flesh, and in the morning ye shall be filled with bread; and ye shall know that I am the LORD your God. And it came to pass, that at even the quails came up, and covered the camp: and in the morning the dew lay round about the host. And when the dew that lay was gone up, behold, upon the face of the wilderness there lay a small round thing, as small as the hoar frost on the ground. And when the children of Israel saw it, they said one to another, It is manna: for they wist not what it was. And Moses said unto them, This is the bread which the LORD hath given you to eat.

**Exodus 16:12-15 NIV** - "I have heard the grumbling of the Israelites. Tell them, 'At twilight you will eat meat, and in the morning you will be filled with bread. Then you will know that I am the LORD your God.' "That evening quail came and covered the camp, and in the morning there was a layer of dew around the camp. When the dew was gone, thin flakes like frost on the ground appeared on the desert floor. W hen the Israelites saw it, they said to each other, "What is it?" For they did not know what it was. Moses said to them, "It is the bread the LORD has given you to eat.

---

[47] Muhammad, *Message to the Blackman*, 155.

You are letting the devils fool and disgrace you and are taking you to hell with them! Your God, Allah, will be happy and will rejoice in feeding, clothing and sheltering you if you believe. The Bible teaches you that He fed and sheltered Israel in the desert (Exod. 16:12-15). Fear not, Allah (God) is with us. The enemies of Allah and the righteous are leading you only to evil and indecency, as the Holy Qur-an teaches you and me.[48]

**Exodus 20:1-18 KJV** - And God spake all these words, saying, I am the LORD thy God, which have brought thee out of the land of Egypt, out of the house of bondage. Thou shalt have no other gods before me. Thou shalt not make unto thee any graven image, or any likeness of anything that is in heaven above, or that is in the earth beneath, or that is in the water under the earth.

Thou shalt not bow down thyself to them, nor serve them: for I the LORD thy God am a jealous God, visiting the iniquity of the fathers upon the children unto the third and fourth generation of them that hate me; And shewing mercy unto thousands of them that love me, and keep my commandments. Thou shalt not take the name of the LORD thy God in vain; for the LORD will not hold him guiltless that taketh his name in vain. Remember the sabbath day, to keep it holy.

Six days shalt thou labour, and do all thy work: But the seventh day is the sabbath of the LORD thy God: in it thou shalt not do any work, thou, nor thy son, nor thy daughter, thy manservant, nor thy maidservant, nor thy cattle, nor

---

[48] Muhammad, *Message to the Blackman*, 101.

thy stranger that is within thy gates: For in six days the LORD made heaven and earth, the sea, and all that in them is, and rested the seventh day: wherefore the LORD blessed the sabbath day, and hallowed it.

Honour thy father and thy mother: that thy days may be long upon the land which the LORD thy God giveth thee. Thou shalt not kill. Thou shalt not commit adultery. Thou shalt not steal. Thou shalt not bear false witness against thy neighbour. Thou shalt not covet thy neighbour's house, thou shalt not covet thy neighbour's wife, nor his manservant, nor his maidservant, nor his ox, nor his ass, nor any thing that is thy neighbour's. And all the people saw the thunderings, and the lightnings, and the noise of the trumpet, and the mountain smoking: and when the people saw it, they removed, and stood afar off.

**Exodus 20:1-18 NIV -** And God spoke all these words: I am the LORD your God, who brought you out of Egypt, out of the land of slavery. "You shall have no other gods before me. You shall not make for yourself an idol in the form of anything in heaven above or on the earth beneath or in the waters below.

You shall not bow down to them or worship them; for I, the LORD your God, am a jealous God, punishing the children for the sin of the fathers to the third and fourth generation of those who hate me, but showing love to a thousand {generations} of those who love me and keep my commandments. "You shall not misuse the name of the LORD your God, for the LORD will not hold anyone guiltless who misuses his name. "Remember the Sabbath day by keeping it holy.

Six days you shall labor and do all your work, but the seventh day is a Sabbath to the LORD your God. On it you shall not do any work, neither you, nor your son or daughter, nor your manservant or maidservant, nor your animals, nor the alien within your gates. For in six days the LORD made the heavens and the earth, the sea, and all that is in them, but he rested on the seventh day. Therefore the LORD blessed the Sabbath day and made it holy.

"Honor your father and your mother, so that you may live long in the land the LORD your God is giving you. "You shall not murder. "You shall not commit adultery. "You shall not steal. "You shall not give false testimony against your neighbor. "You shall not covet your neighbor's house. You shall not covet your neighbor's wife, or his manservant or maidservant, his ox or donkey, or anything that belongs to your neighbor." When the people saw the thunder and lightning and heard the trumpet and saw the mountain in smoke, they trembled with fear.

> **HEM-** The Bible's first five books (or Old Testament) are said to be Moses' Books. But it only mentions the giving of the Ten Commandments, and not a Book (Exodus 20:1-18). I hope that you will not misunderstand me and think that I do not believe in Moses receiving the Torah. Nor does the New Testament open by saying: "This is a book or scripture revealed to Jesus," nor does Jesus tell us that He received a book. But yet the New Testament was revealed to Jesus, and the Revelation (the last Book of

the Bible) was revealed to Yakub (titled John). The Bible being tampered with by the Jews and the Christians has caused many divisions among the people because of their not understanding it. Since the creation of the white race, scripture after scripture along with many prophets have been given to the people of this world for the purpose of guiding and warning the righteous of their enemies, the devils.[49]

**Exodus 32:4 KJV** - And he received them at their hand, and fashioned it with a graving tool, after he had made it a molten calf: and they said, These be thy gods, O Israel, which brought thee up out of the land of Egypt.

**Exodus 32:4 NIV** - He took what they handed him and made it into an idol cast in the shape of a calf, fashioning it with a tool. Then they said, "These are your gods, O Israel, who brought you up out of Egypt.

> **HEM-** Both Jews and Christians are guilty of setting up rivals to Allah (God). Adam and Eve accepted the guidance of the serpent instead of that of Allah (Gen 3:6). They made a golden calf and took it for their god and bowed down to it. This was the work of their own hands to guide them and fight their wars. The Christians have made imaginary pictures and statues of wood, silver and gold- calling them pictures and statues of God. [50]

---

[49] Muhammad, *Message to the Blackman*, 90.
[50] Ibid., 74

# Chapter III:

## Leviticus

Leviticus receives its name from the Septuagint (the pre-Christian Greek translation of the OT) and means "relating to the Levites." Its Hebrew title, *wayyiqra'*, is the first word in the Hebrew text of the book and means "And he [i.e., the Lord] called." Although Leviticus does not deal only with the special duties of the Levites, it is so named because it concerns mainly the service of worship at the tabernacle, which was conducted by the priests who were the sons of Aaron, assisted by many from the rest of the tribe of Levi. Exodus gave the directions for building the tabernacle, and now Leviticus gives the laws and regulations for worship there, including instructions on ceremonial cleanness, moral laws, holy days, the sabbath year and the Year of Jubilee. These laws were given, at least for the most part, during the year that Israel camped at Mount Sinai, when God directed Moses in organizing Israel's worship, government and military forces. The book of Numbers continues the history with preparations for moving on from Sinai to Canaan.[51]

**Leviticus 11:7-8 KJV-** And the swine, though he divide the hoof, and be cloven footed, yet he cheweth not the cud; he is unclean to you. Of their flesh shall ye not eat, and their carcase shall ye not touch; they are unclean to you.

**Leviticus 11:7-8 NIV-** And the pig, though it has a split hoof completely divided, does not chew the cud; it is

---

[51] R. Laird Harris and Ronald Youngblood, *Introduction: Leviticus*, in *New International Version Study Bible* (Grand Rapids, MI: Zondervan, 2002), 146.

unclean for you. You must not eat their meat or touch their carcasses; they are unclean for you.

> **HEM-** God in the Bible, through his prophets, has condemned the eating of the poisonous animal (swine). Leviticus 11:7-8 'And the swine, though he divide the hoof, and be cloven-footed, yet he cheweth not the cud; he is unclean to you. Of their flesh shall ye not eat, and their carcass shall ye not touch; they are unclean to you.' This dietary law given to Israel by Moses is true today. Israel was given the proper food to eat Jehovah approved for them, and that which was forbidden to eat we should not eat today. The Christians have said that since Jesus the swine is good to eat, because Jesus made it good in his teachings. But this is all false and a shield for the Christians' eating the divinely-prohibited flesh of the filthy swine. They even teach you that he has a poison in his flesh.[52]

> **HEM-** Pork is often referred to as "cured." The world "cured" is the past tense of the verb "cure." If a meat has to be cured before we eat it, we should not even take the chance to eat it. In the Bible and the Holy Qur'an, it is the Divine will of God that the pig should not be eaten and God has never changed this instruction, despite the white man's setting up governmental bureaus to grade and approve the selling of pork. The so-called Negroes should ban this meat from their communities and all those who sell and eat it! [53]

---

[52] Muhammad, *How to Eat to Live, Book One,* 95.

[53] Muhammad, *How to Eat to Live, Book Two,* 114.

**HEM-** It is useless to keep repeating to you the same truth day and night, month after month, and year after year when you have it written in your book, the Bible. The main meat that our people like to eat is what they have been taught not to eat- the cheap and filthily-raised hog. This is a divinely-prohibited flesh. This truth has been before our eyes ever since we have had permission from the white man to read the Bible. Nothing good is said about it in the Bible in Leviticus. The priests of Israel were warned not only against the eating of this prohibited, poisonous flesh, but that they should not even touch the carcass. But now the Christians, who claim they are better than all the religious people of the earth, not only touch the carcass, but eat the carcass- and then advise you and others to do the same.[54]

---

[54] Muhammad, *How to Eat to Live, Book One*, 69.

# Chapter IV:

## Numbers

The English name of the book comes from the Septuagint (the pre-Christian Greek translation of the OT) and is based on the census lists found in chs. 1; 26. The Hebrew title of the book (*bemidbar*, "in the desert") is more descriptive of its contents. Numbers presents an account of the 38-year period of Israel's wandering in the desert following the establishment of the covenant of Sinai.

The book has traditionally been ascribed to Moses. This conclusion is based on (1) statements concerning Moses' writing activity (e.g., 33:1–2; Ex 17:14; 24:4; 34:27) and (2) the assumption that the first five books of the Bible, the Pentateuch, are a unit and come from one author. See Introduction to Genesis: Author and Date of Writing. It is not necessary, however, to claim that Numbers came from Moses' hand complete and in final form. Portions of the book were probably added by scribes or editors from later periods of Israel's history. For example, the protestation of the humility of Moses (12:3) would hardly be convincing if it came from his own mouth. But it seems reasonable to assume that Moses wrote the essential content of the book.[55]

**Numbers 12:10-12 KJV-** And the cloud departed from off the tabernacle; and, behold, Miriam became leprous, white as snow: and Aaron looked upon Miriam, and, behold, she

---

[55] Ronald B. Allen and Kenneth L. Baker, *Introduction: Numbers*, in *New International Version Study Bible* (Grand Rapids, MI: Zondervan, 2002), 185.

was leprous. And Aaron said unto Moses, Alas, my lord, I beseech thee, lay not the sin upon us, wherein we have done foolishly, and wherein we have sinned. Let her not be as one dead, of whom the flesh is half consumed when he cometh out of his mother's womb.

**Numbers 12:10 -12 NIV-** When the cloud lifted from above the Tent, there stood Miriam—leprous, like snow. Aaron turned toward her and saw that she had leprosy; and he said to Moses, "Please, my lord, do not hold against us the sin we have so foolishly committed. Do not let her be like a stillborn infant coming from its mother's womb with its flesh half eaten away.

> **HEM-** Fasting is one of the greatest 'doctors' we have. Fasting is prescribed for us in the Holy Qur'an and in the Bible. The Bible does not teach us as much of how good fasting is health-wise, as the Holy Qur'an does. The Bible's teaching on fasting is mostly spiritual purposes. On one occasion, we find where Moses fasted for the cure of his sister, Miriam, who had contracted leprosy because of speaking carelessly of Moses. Her brother (Moses) then had to seek a cure from God for her. (Numbers 12:10-12) But fasting as Allah prescribed for us is to prolong our lives with better health by eating the right food and not eating too frequently.[56]

**Numbers 22:23-26 KJV -** And the ass saw the angel of the LORD standing in the way, and his sword drawn in his hand: and the ass turned aside out of the way, and went into the field: and Balaam smote the ass, to turn her into

---

[56] Muhammad, *How to Eat to Live, Book One,* 45-46.

the way. But the angel of the LORD stood in a path of the vineyards, a wall being on this side, and a wall on that side. And when the ass saw the angel of the LORD, she thrust herself unto the wall, and crushed Balaam's foot against the wall: and he smote her again. And the angel of the LORD went further, and stood in a narrow place, where was no way to turn either to the right hand or to the left.

**Numbers 22:23-26 NIV-** When the donkey saw the angel of the LORD standing in the road with a drawn sword in his hand, she turned off the road into a field. Balaam beat her to get her back on the road. Then the angel of the LORD stood in a narrow path between two vineyards, with walls on both sides. When the donkey saw the angel of the LORD, she pressed close to the wall, crushing Balaam's foot against it. So he beat her again. Then the angel of the LORD moved on ahead and stood in a narrow place where there was no room to turn, either to the right or to the left.

> **HEM-** The foolish still are foolish until he is cast into a narrow place and cannot turn to the right or left, as it was with the donkey that Baalam was riding. He came to a narrow place between two walls. He could not turn around. He had to stop face to face with the angel or be destroyed. Bible Nu. 22:23-26. Let it be remembered that Allah (God) came forth for the Redemption (to Deliver) the American Black People from their tormentors. Whether we like it or not, He Will Do This. This is the work of Allah (God) which is in effect.[57]

---

[57] Muhammad, *The Fall of America*, 213.

# Chapter V:

## Deuteronomy

The Hebrew name of the book is *'elleh haddebarim* ("These are the words") or, more simply, *debarim* ("words"; see 1:1). The word "Deuteronomy" (meaning "repetition of the law") arose from a mistranslation in the Septuagint (the pre-Christian Greek translation of the OT) and the Latin Vulgate of a phrase in Dt 17:18, which in Hebrew means "copy of this law." The error is not serious, however, since Deuteronomy is, in a certain sense, a "repetition of the law". [58]

**Deuteronomy 11:16 KJV-** Take heed to yourselves, that your heart be not deceived, and ye turn aside, and serve other gods, and worship them.

**Deuteronomy 11:16 NIV-** Be careful, or you will be enticed to turn away and worship other gods and bow down to them.

> **HEM-** The American so-called Negroes are gravely deceived by their slave-master's teaching of God and the true religion of God. They do not know that they are deceived and do earnestly believe that they are taught right regardless of how evil the white race may be. Not knowing "self" or anyone else, they are a prey in the hands of the white race, the world's arch deceivers (the real devils in person). You are made to

---

[58] Kenneth L. Baker and Earl S. Kalland, *Introduction: Deuteronomy*, in *New International Version Study Bible* (Grand Rapids, MI: Zondervan, 2002), 241.

believe that you worship the true God, but you do not! God is unknown to you in that which the white race teaches you (a mystery God).[59]

**Deuteronomy 14:8 KJV-** And the swine, because it divideth the hoof, yet cheweth not the cud, it is unclean unto you: ye shall not eat of their flesh, nor touch their dead carcase.

**Deuteronomy 14:8 NIV-** The pig is also unclean; although it has a split hoof, it does not chew the cud. You are not to eat their meat or touch their carcasses.

> **HEM-** In the Bible and the Holy Qur'an, it is the Divine will of God that the pig should not be eaten and God has never changed this instruction, despite the white man's setting up governmental bureaus to grade and approve the selling of pork. [60]

**Deuteronomy 18:15 KJV-** The LORD thy God will raise up unto thee a Prophet from the midst of thee, of thy brethren, like unto me; unto him ye shall hearken;

**Deuteronomy 18:15 NIV -** The LORD your God will raise up for you a prophet like me from among your own brothers. You must listen to him.

> **HEM-** They forget that the Bible prophesies of a lost member of the nation of the original people of the earth, who would be lost somewhere on the earth. But neither the Bible nor the Holy Qur-an specifies the

---

[59] Muhammad, *Message to the Blackman*, 8-9.

[60] Muhammad, *How to Eat to Live II*, 114. See also Leviticus 11:7-8 and Mark 5:13.

place. The nearest the Bible comes to it is that they would be lost in the wilderness. That fits America. And Moses says that God told him (Deut. 18:18) 'I will raise them up a prophet from among thy brethren like unto thee and will put my words in his mouth and shall speak unto them all that I command him.[61]

**HEM-** The problem between these two people -- separating and dignifying the so-called Negroes so they may be accepted and respected as equals or superiors to other nations -- must be solved. This is God's promise to the so-called Negro (the Lost and Found members of the original Black Nation of the earth). This promise was made through the mouths of His prophets (Bible and Qur'an): that He would separate us from our enemies, dignify and make us the masters, after this wicked race has been judged and destroyed for its own evils. But, as I said, the solving of this problem -- which means the redemption of the Negro -- is hard to do since he loves his enemies. (See Bible: Deut., 18:15, 18; Psalms, Isaiah, Matthews, 25:32; and Revelations, Chapter 14.) The manifestation of Allah and judgment between the so-called Negro and the enemy of God and the Nation of Islam will make the so-called Negro see and know his enemy and himself; his people, his God and his religion.[62]

**Deuteronomy 18:18 KJV -** I will raise them up a Prophet from among their brethren, like unto thee, and will put my words in his mouth; and he shall speak unto them all that I shall command him.

---

[61] Muhammad, *Message to the Blackman*, 250.
[62] Muhammad, *The Fall of America*, 158.

**Deuteronomy 18:18 NIV -** I will raise up for them a prophet like you from among their brothers; I will put my words in his mouth, and he will tell them everything I command him.

> **HEM-** This is an answer or a prophecy that compares with the prayer of Abraham- that God raised up a messenger from among them and taught him the wisdom and the book, because his people would not have knowledge of the book and were only guessing at its meaning. This book is referring to the Bible- that they were guessing at its meaning. This is true! Thousands of preachers here are preaching the Bible and do not understand the true meaning of it. They only guess at its meaning.[63]

**Deuteronomy 18:15 KJV-** And of Dan he said, Dan is a lion's whelp: he shall leap from Bashan.

**Deuteronomy 18:15 NIV-** About Dan he said: "Dan is a lion's cub, springing out of Bashan.

> **HEM-** Moses calls Dan a lion's whelp; he shall leap from Bashan; That old serpent, devil and Satan, the old beast, is the dragon which deceiveth the whole world of the poor ignorant darker nations and has caused them to fall off their mount of prosperity, success and independence by accepting advice, guidance and empty promises which he (the serpent-like Caucasian devil) never intended to fulfill.[64]

---

[63] Muhammad, *Message to the Blackman*, 250.

[64] Ibid., 123. Also see 28. Dan is described as a Serpent and the Honorable Elijah Muhammad describes its nature in relation to the Caucasian.

# Chapter VI:

## I Kings

1 and 2 Kings (like 1 and 2 Samuel and 1 and 2 Chronicles) are actually one literary work, called in Hebrew tradition simply "Kings." The division of this work into two books was introduced by the translators of the Septuagint (the pre-Christian Greek translation of the OT) and subsequently followed in the Latin Vulgate (c. a.d. 400) and most modern versions. In 1448 the division into two sections also appeared in a Hebrew manuscript and was perpetuated in later printed editions of the Hebrew text. Both the Septuagint and the Latin Vulgate further designated Samuel and Kings in a way that emphasized the relationship of these two works (Septuagint: First, Second, Third and Fourth Book of Kingdoms; Latin Vulgate: First, Second, Third and Fourth Kings). Together Samuel and Kings relate the whole history of the monarchy, from its rise under the ministry of Samuel to its fall at the hands of the Babylonians.

The division between 1 and 2 Kings has been made at a somewhat arbitrary and yet appropriate place, shortly after the deaths of Ahab of the northern kingdom (22:37) and Jehoshaphat of the southern kingdom (22:50). Placing the division at this point causes the account of the reign of Ahaziah of Israel to overlap the end of 1 Kings (22:51–53) and the beginning of 2 Kings (ch. 1). The same is true of the narration of the ministry of Elijah, which for the most part appears in 1 Kings (chs. 17–19). However, his final act of judgment and the passing of his cloak to Elisha at the moment of his ascension to heaven in a whirlwind are contained in 2 Kings (1:1—2:17). [65]

**I Kings 19:10 KJV** - And he said, I have been very _jealous_ for the LORD God of hosts: for the children of Israel have forsaken thy covenant, thrown down thine altars, and slain thy prophets with the sword; and I, even I only, am left; and they seek my life, to take it away.

**I Kings 19:10 NIV** - He replied, "I have been very _zealous_ for the LORD God Almighty. The Israelites have rejected your covenant, broken down your altars, and put your prophets to death with the sword. I am the only one left, and now they are trying to kill me too."

> **HEM-** Certainly they hate me for teaching you. Certainly they hated all the Messengers of God (Prophets) (I Kings 19:10). The Bible teaches you their history and tells of the denunciation of them from being the killers of the Prophets of God and we see this made manifest today in my work among you. The white man is always planning my death because they hate the truth. The truth makes manifest their evil deeds, against you. They are angry and therefore the spreading of evil is from the angry people of Christiandoom.[66]

---

[65] J. Robert Vannoy, *Introduction: I Kings* in *New International Version Study Bible* (Grand Rapids, MI: Zondervan, 2002), 465.

[66] Muhammad, *Our Saviour Has Arrived*, 202. In the KJV the word *Jealous* קַנָּא (kan·nä') is used. In the NIV the word *Zealous* is used. Zeal קִנְאָה (ze-ree-ZOOT) in its singular noun form means enthusiasm; eagerness to serve or passion. *"Qanna"* in the Septuagint: *zēlōtēs* — jealous. See <http://blueletterbible.org/study/misc/name_god.html>. קַנָּא m., jealous; used of God bearing any rival; the severe avenger of departure from himself; See, Blue Letter Bible. "Dictionary and Word Search for *qanna' (Strong's 7067)*". Blue Letter Bible. 1996-2010. http://www.blueletterbible.org/lang/lexicon/lexicon.cfm?Strongs=H07067&t=KJV

# Chapter VII:

## I Chronicles

The Hebrew title (*dibre hayyamim*) can be translated "the events (or annals) of the days (or years)." The same phrase occurs in references to sources used by the author or compiler of Kings (translated "annals" in, e.g., 1Ki 14:19,29; 15:7,23,31; 16:5,14,20,27; 22:45). The Septuagint (the pre-Christian Greek translation of the OT) refers to the book as "the things omitted," indicating that its translators regarded it as a supplement to Samuel and Kings. Jerome (a.d. 347–420), translator of the Latin Vulgate, suggested that a more appropriate title would be "chronicle of the whole sacred history." Luther took over this suggestion in his German version, and others have followed him. Chronicles was first divided into two books by the Septuagint translators. [67]

**I Chronicles 1:36 KJV -** The sons of Eliphaz; Teman, and Omar, Zephi, and Gatam, Kenaz, and Timna, and Amalek.

**I Chronicles 1:36 NIV-** The sons of Eliphaz: Teman, Omar, Zepho, Gatam and Kenaz; by Timna: Amalek.

> **HEM-** According to the dictionary of the Bible: Teman, a son of Esau by Adah, (Gen. 36:11, 15, 42) and in 1 Chron. 1:36, now if Habakkuk saw God come or coming from the sons of Esau (Eliphaz), then God must be a man and not a spook. If Habakkuk's (3:3) prophecy refers to some country, town, or city, if there

---

[67] Raymond Dillard, *Introduction: I Chronicles* in *New International Version Study Bible* (Grand Rapids, MI: Zondervan, 2002), 577.

be any truth at all in this prophecy, then we can say that this prophet saw God as a material being belonging to the human family of the earth- and not to a spirit (ghost). In the same chapter and verse, Habakkuk saw the Holy One from Mount Paran. This is also earthly, somewhere in Arabia.[68]

---

[68] Muhammad, *Message to the Blackman*, 7.

# Chapter VIII:

## II Chronicles

**II Chronicles 6:31-39 KJV-** That they may fear thee, to walk in thy ways, so long as they live in the land which thou gavest unto our fathers. Moreover concerning the stranger, which is not of thy people Israel, but is come from a far country for thy great name's sake, and thy mighty hand, and thy stretched out arm; if they come and pray in this house; Then hear thou from the heavens, even from thy dwelling place, and do according to all that the stranger calleth to thee for; that all people of the earth may know thy name, and fear thee, as doth thy people Israel, and may know that this house which I have built is called by thy name.

If thy people go out to war against their enemies by the way that thou shalt send them, and they pray unto thee toward this city which thou hast chosen, and the house which I have built for thy name; Then hear thou from the heavens their prayer and their supplication, and maintain their cause. If they sin against thee, (for there is no man which sinneth not,) and thou be angry with them, and deliver them over before their enemies, and they carry them away captives unto a land far off or near; Yet if they bethink themselves in the land whither they are carried captive, and turn and pray unto thee in the land of their captivity, saying, We have sinned, we have done amiss, and have dealt wickedly.

If they return to thee with all their heart and with all their soul in the land of their captivity, whither they have carried them captives, and pray toward their land, which thou gavest unto their fathers, and toward the city which thou hast chosen, and toward the house which I have built for thy name: Then hear thou from the heavens, even from thy dwelling place, their prayer and their supplications, and maintain their cause, and forgive thy people which have sinned against thee.

**II Chronicles 6:31-36 NIV-** So that they will fear you and walk in your ways all the time they live in the land you gave our fathers. As for the foreigner who does not belong to your people Israel but has come from a distant land because of your great name and your mighty hand and your outstretched arm—when he comes and prays toward this temple, then hear from heaven, your dwelling place, and do whatever the foreigner asks of you, so that all the peoples of the earth may know your name and fear you, as do your own people Israel, and may know that this house I have built bears your Name.

When your people go to war against their enemies, wherever you send them, and when they pray to you toward this city you have chosen and the temple I have built for your Name, then hear from heaven their prayer and their plea, and uphold their cause. When they sin against you—for there is no one who does not sin—and you become angry with them and give them over to the enemy, who takes them captive to a land far away or near; and if they have a change of heart in the land where they are held captive, and repent and plead with you in the land of their captivity and say, 'We have sinned, we have done wrong and acted wickedly'; and if they turn back to you with all their heart and soul in the land of their captivity where they were taken, and pray toward the land you gave their fathers, toward the city you have chosen and toward the temple I have built for your Name; then from heaven, your dwelling place, hear their prayer and their pleas, and uphold their cause. And forgive your people, who have sinned against you.

> **HEM-** It is a prayer for forgiveness that Solomon advised you and me to make to Allah if we be lost from our own under the name of Israel. Solomon was a Muslim prophet and king. He and his father David were of the black nation. He advised us to pray toward our own land and toward the Holy City (Mecca) which He has chosen. [69]

---

[69] Muhammad, *Message to the Blackman*, 138.

# Chapter IX:

# Job

Although most of the book consists of the words of Job and his friends, Job himself was not the author. We may be sure that the author was an Israelite, since he (not Job or his friends) frequently uses the Israelite covenant name for God (Yahweh; NIV "the Lord"). In the prologue (chs. 1–2), divine discourses (38:1—42:6) and epilogue (42:7–17) "Lord" occurs a total of 25 times, while in the rest of the book (chs. 3–37) it appears only once (12:9). This unknown author probably had access to a tradition (oral or written) about an ancient righteous man who endured great suffering with remarkable "perseverance" (Jas 5:11; see note there) and without turning against God (see Eze 14:14,20), a tradition he put to use for his own purposes. While the author preserves much of the archaic and non-Israelite flavor in the language of Job and his friends, he also reveals his own style as a writer of wisdom literature. The book's profound insights, its literary structures and the quality of its rhetoric display the author's genius. [70]

**Job 38:22-23 KJV-** Hast thou entered into the treasures of the snow? Or hast thou seen the treasures of the hail, Which I have reserved against the time of trouble, against the day of battle and war?

---

[70] Elmer B. Smick and Ronald Youngblood, *Introduction: Job* in *New International Version Study Bible* (Grand Rapids, MI: Zondervan, 2002), 726.

**Job 38:22-23 NIV-** "Have you entered the storehouses of the snow or seen the storehouses of the hail, which I reserve for times of trouble, for days of war and battle?"

> **HEM-** Snow is prophesied to be one of the weapons that God will use against the wicked (America), Job 38:22, Hail also is mentioned in the same two verses, where God plainly tells us that He has preserved it against the time of trouble, against the day of the battle and war. The Holy Qur'an also teaches us that God used snow, rain, wind, hail, earthquakes and fire against former wicked people.[71]

> **HEM-** The four mentioned weapons of Allah (God) cannot be ignored. The whole year has been a year thus far of Allah (God) plaguing America day and night with storms, rains, floods; killing and destroying property. And now the coming winter -- hail has been falling in some places the size of golf balls, baseballs and footballs. The rain continues to fall in places and a dreadful snow blizzard is now in the workings. A cold wind is brewing in the North to come against America, as it is written and prophesied in Job 38:22-23: "Hast thou entered into the treasures of the snow? Or has thou seen the treasures of the hail, which I have reserved against the time of trouble, against the day of battle and war?"[72]

---

[71] Muhammad, *The Fall of America*, 158.
[72] Ibid., 196.

# Chapter X:

# Psalms

The titles "Psalms" and "Psalter" come from the Septuagint (the pre-Christian Greek translation of the OT), where they originally referred to stringed instruments (such as harp, lyre and lute), then to songs sung with their accompaniment. The traditional Hebrew title is *tehillim* (meaning "praises"; see note on Ps 145 title), even though many of the psalms are *tephillot* (meaning "prayers"). In fact, one of the first collections included in the book was titled "the prayers of David son of Jesse" (72:20). [73]

**HEM-** The Psalmist teaches you and me that the names of the white race have no meaning and value of good. They are not the Names of God; therefore these names of the white race and the people who go in such names as Wood, Fish, and Bear will be removed. The people of Righteousness will not be called by such names. Imagine you're being called Mr. Briar! You are not a Briar or Mr. Fish; you are not a Fish. These names are worthless to be used as names of human beings.[74]

**HEM-** The sign in the Bible by David (Psalms) limits the life of the wicked to *three score and 10 years (seventy years)* and in another place (In the Psalms) he says that the wicked live not half their days.[75]

---

[73] John H. Stek, *Introduction: Psalm* in *New International Version Study Bible* (Grand Rapids, MI: Zondervan, 2002), 778.
[74] Muhammad, Elijah. *Our Saviour Has Arrive*, 126.
[75] Muhammad, *How to Eat to Live, Book Two,* 131.

## Psalms 2

> **HEM-** It should be clear to you today that Christian America does not want such preaching as entire submission to the will of Allah (Islam). The Christians hate the very names of God: such as Muhammad, Omar, Karriem, Ali, Hassan, which are attributes of God. The Jesus prophesied that they would hate you for His (God's) name sake, for having one of His names, because the names of God are to live forever. No other people on earth have the names of God but the Muslims. So the coming of the Just One makes manifest to you this evil race of sinners. And they will be against His (God's) presence; be angered because of Him and will seek to destroy Him and His messenger as it is prophesied.[76]

**Psalms 2:4 KJV-** He that sitteth in the heavens shall laugh: the LORD shall have them in derision.

**Psalms 2:4 NIV-** The One enthroned in heaven laughs; the Lord scoffs at them.

> **HEM-** The rich, the wealthy and powerful rulers of America, from the mayors of cities, the police commissioners up to the President work to oppose the Black once-slave's return to his own. All of this hastens their doom, as the Bible, Ps. 2:4, teaches us, "He that sitteth in the heavens shall laugh: the Lord shall have them in derision."[77]

---

[76] Muhammad, *The Fall of America*, 58.
[77] Ibid., 126

**Psalms 10:8 KJV-** He sitteth in the lurking places of the villages: in the secret places doth he murder the innocent: his eyes are privily set against the poor.

**Psalms 10:8 NIV-** He lies in wait near the villages; from ambush he murders the innocent, watching in secret for his victims.

> **HEM-** It is very sad and horrible to look at the things that America had done, which are now coming on this country. For many years -- centuries of years, America has lived a luxurious, wicked life, while hating her Black slaves and depriving them of justice -- shooting them down on the streets, on the highways and in the woods and fields, for nothing. She did it just because she felt that she had the advantage; and she wanted to kill Black people, as she was made to do. Bible Ps. 10:8, "He sitteth in the lurking places of the villages: in the secret places doth he murder the innocent: his eyes are set against the poor." Up until this very minute, she is seeking to destroy the Black man in America and to deprive him of the freedom to do for self. America never desires a departure of the Black slave from his white slave-master. America wishes only to hold the Black slave in order to continue to treat him with evil.[78]

**Psalms 29:11 KJV-** The LORD will give strength unto his people; the LORD will bless his people with peace.

**Psalms 29:11 NIV-** 35:8, The LORD gives strength to his people; the LORD blesses his people with peace.

---

[78] Muhammad, *The Fall of America*, 161.

> **HEM-** The significance of the name "Islam" is peace, the true religion. It is the religion of eternal peace. We cannot image Allah (God) offering to us a religion other than one off peace. A religion of peace coming to the righteous after the destruction of the wicked is also mentioned in several places in the Bible: "The Lord will bless His people with peace.(Psa. 29:11)" " He will speak peace unto His people and to His saints (Psa. 35:8) and "the Lord of Peace give you peace always" (II Thess. 3:16).[79]

**Psalms 35:8 KJV-** Let destruction come upon him at unawares; and let his net that he hath hid catch himself: into that very destruction let him fall.

**Psalms 35:8 NIV-** May ruin overtake them by surprise- may the net they hid entangle them, may they fall into the pit, to their

**Psalms 37:32 KJV-** The wicked watcheth the righteous, and seeketh to slay him.

**Psalms 37:32 NIV-** The wicked lie in wait for the righteous, seeking their very lives.

> **HEM-** They (the devils) watch the steps of the righteous (the Negroes) and seek to slay them (Psalms 37:32). The so-called Negroes live under the very shadow of death in America. There is no justice for them in the courts of their slave-masters. Why should not America be chastised for her evils done to the so-called Negroes? If God destroyed ancient Babylon for

---

[79] Muhammad, *Message to the Blackman*, 69-70.

the mockery made of the sacred vessels taken from the Temple in Jerusalem, what do you think Allah (God) should do for America's mockery of the so-called Negroes -- that she took from their native land and people and filled them with wine and whiskey.[80]

**Psalms 68:30 KJV-** Rebuke the company of spearmen, the multitude of the bulls, with the calves of the people, till every one submit himself with pieces of silver: scatter thou the people that delight in war.

**Psalms 68:30 NIV-** Rebuke the beast among the reeds, the herd of bulls among the calves of the nations. Humbled, may it bring bars of silver. Scatter the nations who delight in war.

> **HEM-** We have past histories that teach us of the fall and rise of many nations. However, in this day -- after this destruction of the nations, there will be no rise of these destroyed nations because Allah (God) Who came in the Person of Master Fard Muhammad to Whom praises are due forever, will destroy those who cause evil to spread far and wide. He will destroy those who love to make war on others, as it is written, Ps. 68:30. During the whole time of the mischief-maker (devil) -- six thousand years on our planet -- there has been one war right after another. There has never been any peace among them. You cannot live with them in peace. Peace was never in the nature of the white race.[81]

---

[80] Muhammad, *Message to the Blackman*, 274.
[81] Muhammad, *The Fall of America*, 120.

**Psalms 94:16 KJV-** Who will rise up for me against the evildoers? Or who will stand up for me against the workers of iniquity?

**Psalms 94:16 NIV -** Who will rise up for me against the wicked? Who will take a stand for me against evildoers?

> **HEM-** Who will rise up for me against the workers of iniquity? I have answered Him and said, "Here I am, take me." For the evil done against my people (the so-called Negroes) I will not keep silent until He executes judgment and defends my cause. Fear not my life, for He is well able to defend it. Know that God is a man and not a spook![82]

**Psalms 94:20-21 KJV-** Shall the throne of iniquity have fellowship with thee, which frameth mischief by a law? They gather themselves together against the soul of the righteous, and condemn the innocent blood.

**Psalms 94:20-21 NIV-** Can a corrupt throne be allied with you - one that brings on misery by its decrees? They band together against the righteous and condemn the innocent to death.

> **HEM-** As David says in his Psalms 94:20: "Shall the throne of iniquity have fellowship with thee, which frameth mischief by a law?" The poor lost-found members of the Tribe of Shabazz (nicknamed "Negroes" by their slave-masters) can well understand that they are the victims of such a frame-up against them throughout America when they seek truth, love

---

[82] Muhammad, *Message to the Blackman*, 10.

and unity among themselves. The white race does not want to see the poor black people of America united in Islam, a religion that is of Allah (God) backed by the spirit and power of God, to unite all of its believers into one nation of brotherhood. It is the only unifying religion known and tried by the races and nations of earth. This the white race knows.[83]

**HEM-** Shall we go back to that which He has brought us out of? No! As it is written: "Shall the throne of iniquity have fellowship with thee, which frameth mischief by a law? They gather themselves together against the soul of the righteous and condemn the innocent blood (the so-called American Negroes) Psalms 94:20-21). And again it teaches, 'Can there be fellowship with light and darkness?" Let the American so-called Negroes return to their Allah and His religion or suffer what was poured upon Pharaoh and his people for their opposition to Moses, the servant of Allah.[84]

**Psalms 106:37 KJV-** Yea, they sacrificed their sons and their daughters unto devils.

**Psalms 106:37 NIV-** They sacrificed their sons and their daughters to demons.

> **HEM-** The Bible warns us against the love and worship of these devils. Psalms 106:37, says "Yea, they sacrificed their sons and their daughters unto devils." In another place it states, "And I would not that you should have fellowship with devils: ye cannot be

---

[83] Muhammad, *Message to the Blackman*, 131.
[84] Muhammad, *Our Saviour Has Arrived*, 73-74.

partakers of the Lord's table and of the table of the devils. (1Cor. 10:21). "They should not worship up devils" (Rev. 9:20).[85]

**Psalm 137:8 KJV-** O daughter of Babylon, who art to be destroyed; happy shall he be, that rewardeth thee as thou hast served us.

**Psalm 137:8 NIV-** O Daughter of Babylon, doomed to destruction, happy is he who repays you for what you have done to us.

> **HEM-** In Psalm 137:8, David prophesies that Babylon was made to be destroyed. We know of nothing other than the devil and his works that was actually made to be destroyed spiritually. The devil was not made to exist forever. This is verified by both the Bible and the Holy Qur'an and by all writers and teachers of scripture. So, here, Babylon seems to refer not only to some town or city, but it also seems to refer to a race or a nation of people.[86]

---

[85] Muhammad, *Message to the Blackman*, 232.

[86] Muhammad, *The Fall of America*, 138.

# Chapter XI:

## Proverbs

Although the book begins with a title ascribing the proverbs to Solomon, it is clear from later chapters that he was not the only author of the book. Pr 22:17 refers to the "sayings of the wise," and 24:23 mentions additional "sayings of the wise." The presence of an introduction in 22:17–21 further indicates that these sections stem from a circle of wise men, not from Solomon himself. Ch. 30 is attributed to Agur son of Jakeh and 31:1–9 to King Lemuel, neither of whom is mentioned elsewhere. Lemuel's sayings contain several Aramaic spellings that may point to a non-Israelite background.[87]

**Proverbs 22:1 KJV-** A GOOD name is rather to be chosen than great riches, and loving favour rather than silver and gold.

**Proverbs 22:1 NIV-** A good name is more desirable than great riches; to be esteemed is better than silver or gold.

> **HEM-** Take a look at the change of names. The Bible teaches us that He Will Accept those who are called by His Name. And some of us are foolish as to say, 'What is in a name?' Everything is in a name. The Bible teaches us that all of these Names of Allah (God) are more valuable than fine gold, because in the Judgment

---

[87] Herbert Wolf, *Introduction: Proverbs* in *New International Version Study Bible* (Grand Rapids, MI: Zondervan, 2002), 954.

they will save your life from being destroyed. All people who do not have a Name of the God of Righteousness and Justice will be destroyed. Read your Bible; it is there in the last Book. Revelations warns you that all who have the name of the beast are pushed into hell fire - all of the beast's disciples or false prophets such as the preachers of the Christian religion and those who are helping the beast to deceive us, as they are deceived. Read your Bible. It teaches us that they were blind teachers who could not lead a seeing one, nor could they lead another blind one; for they are blind themselves.[88]

**Proverbs 23:7 KJV-** For as he thinketh in his heart, so is he: Eat and drink, saith he to thee; but his heart is not with thee.

**Proverbs 23:7 NIV-** For he is the kind of man who is always thinking about the cost. "Eat and drink," he says to you, but his heart is not with you.

> **HEM-** This Christ Who is referred to in the above verse is Allah (God) in Person (The Mahdi). This is true and the scriptures prophecy teaches you that You have to be new to be one of His followers. He changes you in mind; and it is written 'as man think, so is he' (Pr. 23:7). Christ the true interpretation of the Name is 'The Crusher.' When understood, It makes the God Coming in the Last Day to Crush the wicked to be the True Answer to that Name of Christ. You call Him the Anointed One that is true. He is Anointed to Crush the wicked. He does Not Come loving the wicked as

---

[88] Muhammad, *Our Saviour Has Arrived*, 78-79.

you would like Him to do since you are wicked yourself.[89]

**Proverbs 29:25 KJV-** The fear of man bringeth a snare: but whoso putteth his trust in the LORD shall be safe.
**Proverbs 29:25 NIV-** Fear of man will prove to be a snare, but whoever trusts in the LORD is kept safe.

> **HEM-** This fear is the fear of the slave-masters (white man) and what the slave-masters dislike. Let the so-called Negroes submit to Allah (God) and they will not fear anymore, nor will they grieve. As it is written: The fear of man bringeth a snare. It has surely snared the so-called Negroes. [90]

---

[89] Muhammad, *Our Saviour Has Arrived*, 128-29.
[90] Muhammad, *Message to the Blackman*, 29.

# Chapter XII:

## Isaiah

In the Hebrew Bible the book of Isaiah initiates a division called the Latter Prophets (for the Former Prophets see Introduction to Joshua: Title and Theological Theme), including also Jeremiah, Ezekiel and the Twelve Minor Prophets (so called because of their small size by comparison with the major prophetic books of Isaiah, Jeremiah and Ezekiel, and not at all suggesting that they are of minor importance; see essay, p. 1341). Thus Isaiah occupies pride of place among the Latter Prophets. This is fitting since he is sometimes referred to as the prince of the prophets.[91]

**Isaiah 8:1 KJV** - Woe to the land shadowing with wings, which is beyond the rivers of Ethiopia.

**Isaiah 8:1 NIV** - Woe to the land of whirring wings along the rivers of Cush.

> **HEM-** Calamity! Calamity in the country of America. No secret can remain hidden, for the chastisement of Allah (God) will not let you hide it. As one writer prophesied in the Bible (Is. 18:1), "Woe to the land shadowing with wings..." This prophesy is referring to America which has a cloud of planes shadowing the skies over America almost daily.[92]

---

[91] John H. Stek and Herbert Wolf, *Introduction: Proverbs* in *New International Version Study Bible* (Grand Rapids, MI: Zondervan, 2002), 1132.
[92] Muhammad, *The Fall of America*, 224.

**Isaiah 9:6 KJV** - For unto us a child is born, unto us a son is given: and the government shall be upon his shoulder: and his name shall be called Wonderful, Counsellor, The mighty God, The everlasting Father, The Prince of Peace.

**Isaiah 9:6 NIV** - For to us a child is born, to us a son is given, and the government will be on his shoulders. And he will be called Wonderful Counselor, Mighty God, Everlasting Father, Prince of Peace.

> **HEM-** Jesus himself said that he was not God. The coming of Jesus was not God. The coming of Jesus was not ever prophesied in the Old Testament of the Bible. What you read of Jesus, in the Old Testament- that is myself: the last days with a government upon his shoulder. Isa. 9:6. Jesus did not have a government upon his shoulder, which is what he needed for a prophet that is to rule, attack, and destroy the Jews, Christians, and Greeks- authorities over religion. He needed that knowledge and power. If he had a government upon his shoulder- what government?[93]

**Isaiah 14:3 KJV** - And it shall come to pass in the day that the LORD shall give thee rest from thy sorrow, and from thy fear, and from the hard bondage wherein thou wast made to serve.

**Isaiah 14:3 NIV-** On the day the LORD gives you relief from suffering and turmoil and cruel bondage, you will take up this taunt against the king of Babylon: How the oppressor has come to an end! How his fury has ended!

---

[93] Muhammad, *Our Saviour Has Arrived*, 146.

**HEM-** There are so many places that I could point out in the Bible and Holy Qur'an that warn us of fearing our enemies above or equal to the fear of Allah (God). It is a fool who has greater fear of the devils (white man) than Allah who has the power to destroy the devils and their followers (Revelation 21:8; Holy Qur'an 7:18 and 15:43). We must remember that if Islam means entire submission to the will of Allah, that and that alone is the True religion of Allah. Do not you and your religious teachers and the Prophets of old teach that the only way to receive God's help or Guidance is to submit to his will! -then WHY NOT ISLAM! It (Islam) is the true religion of Allah and the ONLY way to success.[94]

**Isaiah 14:13, 16 KJV-** For thou hast said in thine heart, I will ascend into heaven, I will exalt my throne above the stars of God: I will sit also upon the mount of the congregation, in the sides of the north. I will ascend above the heights of the clouds; I will be like the most High. Yet thou shalt be brought down to hell, to the sides of the pit. They that see thee shall narrowly look upon thee, and consider thee, saying, Is this the man that made the earth to tremble, that did shake kingdoms.

**Isaiah 14:13, 16 NIV-** You said in your heart, "I will ascend to heaven; I will raise my throne above the stars of God; I will sit enthroned on the mount of assembly, on the utmost heights of the sacred mountain. I will ascend above the tops of the clouds; I will make myself like the Most High." But you are brought down to the grave, to the depths of the pit. Those who see you stare at you, they ponder your

---

[94] Muhammad, *Message to the Blackman*, 29.

fate: "Is this the man who shook the earth and made kingdoms tremble.

> **HEM-** Man is easily made, but the sun, moon and stars are much harder to make. Yet we are the makers of them. In making the moon, it was not our original father's intention to make the moon as it is. His real intention was to destroy the moon (earth) but failed and all others who make such attempts will fail. What! You disbelieve it? Do you not see that the devils are trying to make themselves a satellite to make you believe that they are the masters of the heaven and the earth, as it is written of them in the Bible and Holy Qur'an.[95]

**Isaiah 14:16-17 KJV-** They that see thee shall narrowly look upon thee, and consider thee, saying, Is this the man that made the earth to tremble, that did shake kingdoms; that made the world as a wilderness, and destroyed the cities thereof; that opened not the house of his prisoners?

**Isaiah 14:16-17 NIV-** Those who see you stare at you, they ponder your fate: "Is this the man who shook the earth and made kingdoms tremble, the man who made the world a desert, who overthrew its cities and would not let his captives go home?"

> **HEM-** Again the Bible teaches us, Is. 59:14 and justice standeth afar off: for truth is fallen in the street.' This is true of America, and yet she looks for peace. How can she find peace when she is guilty of breaking the peace of the world and refusing to let her prisoners

---

[95] Muhammad, *Message to the Blackman*,109-110.

(so-called Negroes) go Is. 14:17. The so-called Negro is too wild. He does not know how to strike to obtain the result of Justice for himself. He is swinging wildly, but still the God is with him to bring to pass that which is written. I say to you, my Black brothers and sisters throughout America, join onto Islam. Follow me and I will lead you into the right way and God will bless you with that which you desire in your heart of good.[96]

**HEM-** Some of the devil's disciples are called "father" after the pope, the chief father of Satan's religion, Christianity. The pope claims in the Bible, that he will sit in the sides of the north and be like the Most High. Isa. 14:13.14. And yet Allah (God) promised to pull him down to hell (Isa. 14:15). And Allah is going to pull him down real fast. The Vatican, the home of the pope, has gotten one of the worst beatings with plagues, snow, ice, and enemies--the worst beatings that you ever could have imagined coming to the head of the church. This shows that Allah (God), the Supreme Being, does not respect Rome and its father whom they call pope. The Vatican, if it were a holy place, we would not expect to suffer the curse of nature. We who live in America live in a cursed country. America is a cursed country. America is a divine place of exile for Allah's enemies and he promises to use America now for a lake of fire in which to burn all of his enemies. The Indians, the first people who were sent--who migrated to America--the Indians were also the enemies of Allah.[97]

---

[96] Muhammad, *Our Saviour Has Arrived*, 206. Included is Isa.14:16. Although not referenced in this book, it helps bring perspective to the Isa. 14:17 and what the Honorable Elijah Muhammad refers to in the above mentioned explanation.

[97] Muhammad, *The Fall of America*, 22.

**Isaiah 18:1 KJV-** Woe to the land shadowing with wings, which is beyond the rivers of Ethiopia.

**Isaiah 18:1 NIV-** Woe to the land of whirring wings along the rivers of Cush.

> **HEM-** The sky over America is shadowed with thousands of planes, but yet the grievous destruction awaits America. America sends planes flying out into space by means of the most modern rockets designed for space-travel! At home, America's country is as the prophet foresaw and prophesied of it; America is covered with planes and her army is standing ready to stop inside rebellion. The prophet who foresaw all of this readiness and preparation for the world showdown of military might, says, "Woe to the land shadowing with wings..." (Bible Is. 18:1). America takes a look around the dead piece of our earth...the moon. She wants to see if they can do her harm. America takes a look at Venus and Mars to see if there are signs of any gods on these planets who are capable of warring with her. America boasts of her ability to kill the civilization of earth three times over and have an army left to attack anywhere else that an enemy may rise up against her.[98]

**Isaiah 24:1 KJV-** Behold, the LORD maketh the earth empty, and maketh it waste, and turneth it upside down, and scattereth abroad the inhabitants thereof.

---

[98] Muhammad, *The Fall of America*, 125.

**Isaiah 24:1 NIV-** See, the LORD is going to lay waste the earth and devastate it; he will ruin its face and scatter its inhabitants.

> **HEM-** In the Days of the Son of Man there will be much trouble and confusion of Nations. Bible Is. 24:1 says the whole earth will be turned upside down and nations scattered abroad.[99]

> **HEM-** Allah (God) Who came in the Person of Master Fard Muhammad, to Whom praises are due forever, is wiser than any god before Him as the Bible and the Holy Qur'an teach us. He taught me that this place will be used to raise mountains on this planet (earth). The mountains that He will put on this earth will not be very high. He will raise these mountains to a height of one (1) mile over the United States of America. This reminds us of the prophet's prediction of this time of the destruction of the old world and the bringing in of a new world: "Behold, the Lord, maketh the earth empty, and maketh it waste, and turneth it upside down, and scattereth aborad the inhabitants thereof." (Bible Is. 24:1)[100]

**Isaiah 24:20 KJV-** The earth shall reel to and fro like a drunkard, and shall be removed like a cottage; and the transgression thereof shall be heavy upon it; and it shall fall, and not rise again.

**Isaiah 24:20 NIV-** The earth reels like a drunkard, it sways like a hut in the wind; so heavy upon it is the guilt of its rebellion that it falls never to rise again.

---

[99] Muhammad, *Our Saviour Has Arrived*, 185-186.
[100] Muhammad, *The Fall of America*, 236.

**HEM-** Space here in this book is limited, but what Allah (God) taught me concerning the Mother Plane could be put into book-form. O wheel, made to rock the earth and to heave up mountains upon the earth. O wheel, destroyer of nations. No wonder the prophet Isaiah prophesied that the "earth shall reel to and fro like a drunkard..." (Bible; Is. 24:20). Let us seek refuge in Allah (God) from the destructive work to come from this Mother of planes.[101]

**Isaiah 29:17-18 KJV-** Is it not yet a very little while, and Lebanon shall be turned into a fruitful field, and the fruitful field shall be esteemed as a forest? And in that day shall the deaf hear the words of the book, and the eyes of the blind shall see out of obscurity, and out of darkness.

**Isaiah 29:17-18 NIV-** In a very short time, will not Lebanon be turned into a fertile field and the fertile field seem like a forest? In that day the deaf will hear the words of the scroll, and out of gloom and darkness the eyes of the blind will see.

> **HEM-** Today the white race, the blacks' worst enemies, has planned to make a last try to destroy the black man by pretending to be their friends and allow intermarriage. Many Americans (especially the Southerners) don't like the idea, but will finally be persuaded by their more learned men when they see no other way of making a final stroke at the black man. It will be

---

[101] Muhammad, *The Fall of America*, 242.

short-lived for the judgment will sit, and the agreement will be broken between the black and whites as it is written.[102]

**Isaiah 43:6 KJV-** I will say to the north, Give up; and to the south, Keep not back: bring my sons from far, and my daughters from the ends of the earth.

**Isaiah 43:6 NIV-** I will say to the north, 'Give them up!' and to the south, 'Do not hold them back.' Bring my sons from afar and my daughters from the ends of the earth.

> **HEM-** Allah (God) comes to take the Black slave away from the enemy white slave-holder and join the Black slave onto his own kind again. The enemy white slave-holder hates this, but Allah (God) has the power to force the enemy white slave-holder to submit to His will. It is the will of Allah (God) that the enemy white slave-holder let the Black slave go free. Allah (God) promises concerning the white slave-holder and the Black slave, Bible Is. 43:6, "I will say to the north, Give up; and to the south, Keep not back: bring my sons from far, and my daughters from the ends of the earth;" (America).[103]

**Isaiah 43:13 KJV-** Yea, before the day was I am he; and there is none that can deliver out of my hand: I will work, and who shall let it?

---

[102] Muhammad, *Message to the Blackman*, 107.
[103] Muhammad, *The Fall of America*, 223.

**Isaiah 43:13 NIV-** Yes, and from ancient days I am he. No one can deliver out of my hand. When I act, who can reverse it?"

> **HEM-** America is spending billions of dollars in a futile attempt to stop the stormy war clouds that are hovering over her concessions but she is not getting at the root cause of it. The reason why the cloud is rising with destruction is because of her so-called Negro slaves whom she refuses to let go. She divides them one against the other for her own sake. It has not proven to be against her own peace because the God of the so-called Negro is on the scene and is Directing His Own Cause, as it is written, Bible, Is. 43:13.[104]

**Isaiah 43:23 KJV-** I have sworn by myself, the word is gone out of my mouth in righteousness, and shall not return, That unto me every knee shall bow, every tongue shall swear.

**Isaiah 43:23 KJV-** By myself I have sworn, my mouth has uttered in all integrity a word that will not be revoked: Before me every knee will bow; by me every tongue will swear.

> **HEM-** Before the time is out, they will be forced into submission to the will of Allah (God). This will not be done for the purpose of converting the white race Allah (God) will force them into submission to prove that He is able to make everything bow to Him in submission. This is in fulfillment to the prophecy, Bible Is. 45-23, "...unto me every knee shall bow; every

---

[104] Muhammad, *Our Saviour Has Arrived*, 206.

tongue shall swear. "The Bible says, Mt. 25:32, "And before Him shall be gathered all nations:...." The Holy Qur'an has a similar prophecy, "that you shall see all nations kneeling before Him." This includes everybody, regardless to their color. Everything in the universe obeys the natural law in which it was made subject to by Allah (God).[105]

**Isaiah 44:25 KJV-** That frustrateth the tokens of the liars, and maketh diviners mad; that turneth wise men backward, and maketh their knowledge foolish.

**Isaiah 44:25 NIV-** Who foils the signs of false prophets and makes fools of diviners, who overthrows the learning of the wise and turns it into nonsense.

> **HEM-** Allah (God) laughs at their struggle to bring to a naught His aims and purpose of freedom, justice and equality to His Black people. Allah (God) has them (heads of America) in derision and confusion to the limit of their wits. In another place, the Bible teaches us, that He (Allah) will turn them backward. (Is. 44:25)[106]

**Isaiah 44:8 KJV-** Fear ye not, neither be afraid: have not I told thee from that time, and have declared it? ye are even my witnesses. Is there a God beside me? yea, there is no God; I know not any.

**Isaiah 44:8 NIV-** Do not tremble, do not be afraid. Did I not proclaim this and foretell it long ago? You are my

---

[105] Muhammad, *The Fall of America*, 215.
[106] Ibid., 126.

witnesses. Is there any God besides me? No, there is no other Rock; I know not one."

**Isaiah 45:22 KJV-** Look unto me, and be ye saved, all the ends of the earth: for I am God, and there is none else.

**Isaiah 45:22 NIV-** Turn to me and be saved, all you ends of the earth; for I am God, and there is no other.

**Isaiah 46:9 KJV-** Remember the former things of old: for I am God, and there is none else; I am God, and there is none like me.

**Isaiah 46:9 NIV-** Remember the former things, those of long ago; I am God, and there is no other; I am God, and there is none like me.

> **HEM-** If Jesus said that he was sent (Matt. 15:24 and John 4:34) then he cannot claim to be equal of His sender. God is not sent by anyone; He is a self-sender. He says in Isaiah (44:81-45:22): "Is there a God besides Me? I know not any.(45:22)" In another place He states "I am God, there is none else.(46:9)" Also, "One God and none other." (Mark 12:32)[107]

**Isaiah 47:1 KJV-** Come down, and sit in the dust, O virgin daughter of Babylon, sit on the ground: there is no throne, O daughter of the Chaldeans: for thou shalt no more be called tender and delicate.

---

[107] Muhammad, *Message to the Blackman*, 27.

**Isaiah 47:1 NIV-** Go down, sit in the dust, Virgin Daughter of Babylon; sit on the ground without a throne, Daughter of the Babylonians. No more will you be called tender or delicate.

> **HEM-** A prophecy relating to America is mentioned in Isaiah (47:1) as a "virgin daughter" of ancient Babylon's history. As we all know, America is the last, the greatest and the richest remaining power of the white nations. But now she is falling and the prophet Isaiah says, "Come and sit down in the dust," humble yourself, for you are no more called delicate.[108]

> **HEM-** In Jeremiah, (Bible) we see a daughter of ancient Babylon. He calls the people "the daughters of ancient Babylon." These people are not the old parents, but they are the daughters from those parents. The daughter of ancient Babylon refers to a later and modern civilization whose people give themselves over to the practice of the same evil that the people of Ancient Babylon practiced. But, the modern people were more capable of improving on the practices of the people of ancient Babylon. Therefore, he calls this modern people "the daughters of ancient Babylon. Isaiah (Bible Is. 47:1) asks this people, the daughter of Babylon, "Come down, and sit in the dust, O virgin daughter of Babylon, sit on the ground: there is no throne....for thou shalt no more be called tender and delicate."[109]

**Isaiah 49:24-26 KJV-** Shall the prey be taken from the mighty, or the lawful captive delivered? But thus saith the

---

[108] Muhammad, *The Fall of America*, 135.
[109] Ibid., 140.

LORD, Even the captives of the mighty shall be taken away, and the prey of the terrible shall be delivered: for I will contend with him that contendeth with thee, and I will save thy children. And I will feed them that oppress thee with their own flesh; and they shall be drunken with their own blood, as with sweet wine: and all flesh shall know that I the LORD am thy Saviour and thy Redeemer, the mighty One of Jacob.

**Isaiah 49:24-26 NIV-** Can plunder be taken from warriors, or captives rescued from the fierce? But this is what the LORD says:"Yes, captives will be taken from warriors, and plunder retrieved from the fierce; I will contend with those who contend with you, and your children I will save. I will make your oppressors eat their own flesh; they will be drunk on their own blood, as with wine. Then all mankind will know that I, the LORD, am your Savior, your Redeemer, the Mighty One of Jacob."

> **HEM-** Shall you (the Non-Muslim world) be the winner in the third World War? The God of Justice (The Son of Man, The Great Mahdi) shall be the winner. He is on the side of the so-called Negroes, to free them from you, their killers. As it is written: "Shall the prey be taken from the mighty or the lawful captives delivered? But this saith the Lord, even the captives of the mighty shall be taken away and the prey of the terrible shall be delivered; for I will contend with him that contendeth with thee. I will feed them that oppress thee with their own flesh; and they shall be drunken with their own blood. As with sweet wine

and all flesh shall know that I, the Lord, am thy Saviour and thy Redeemer"[110]

**HEM-** The so-called Negroes are the prey (Isa. 49:24) of the mighty United States as Israel was in the days of Pharaoh. They were a prey under the power of Pharaoh. According to the Bible, they had nothing like a share in the land of Egypt. A few cattle and the land or home given to Joseph's father house in the days of Joseph all seemed to have disappeared in the time of Moses. Jehovah appeared to Moses in the bush. Moses was made to see the bush in a flame of fire though there was no actual fire. The fire represented the anger of Jehovah against Pharaoh and his people. It was a declaration of a divine war against the Egyptians for the deliverance of Israel.[111]

## Isaiah Chapter 53

**HEM-** Do not look at me when you see me sick. This suffering is what I have to go through with to prove myself worthy of being, the Last Messenger of Allah. I am afflicted with everything that you are afflicted with. According to the Bible, Isaiah, Chapter 53, 'In all of your afflictions he was afflicted.' Allah (God) wants to show you in the example that He makes of me, that I have suffered the same afflictions that you have, so that you will not have this as an excuse for your disbelieving. You cannot claim that I did not suffer the same things that you suffered, that God Would Not Have Found me to be the good Messenger. I suffer sickness with you. I suffered imprisonment with you. I suffered the deprivation of family as you have. Show

---

[110] Muhammad, *Message to the Blackman*, 299.
[111] Muhammad, *Our Saviour Has Arrived*, 18.

me what you have suffered, that I have not suffered. It is necessary for the Last Messenger to suffer a taste of what all of the prophets before him suffered. Therefore, the Last Messenger is called the fulfillment of the prophets. He fulfills the same history of the former prophets...except death. He is not to be murdered...God Will Not Suffer that.[112]

**Isaiah 56:1-5 KJV-** Thus saith the LORD, Keep ye judgment, and do justice: for my salvation is near to come, and my righteousness to be revealed. Blessed is the man that doeth this, and the son of man that layeth hold on it; that keepeth the sabbath from polluting it, and keepeth his hand from doing any evil. Neither let the son of the stranger, that hath joined himself to the LORD, speak, saying, The LORD hath utterly separated me from his people: neither let the eunuch say, Behold, I am a dry tree. For thus saith the LORD unto the eunuchs that keep my sabbaths, and choose the things that please me, and take hold of my covenant; Even unto them will I give in mine house and within my walls a place and a name better than of sons and of daughters: I will give them an everlasting name, that shall not be cut off.

**Isaiah 56:1-5 NIV-** This is what the LORD says: "Maintain justice and do what is right, for my salvation is close at hand and my righteousness will soon be revealed. Blessed is the man who does this, the man who holds it fast, who keeps the Sabbath without desecrating it, and keeps his hand from doing any evil. "Let no foreigner who has bound himself to the LORD say, "The LORD will surely

---

[112] Muhammad, *How to Eat to Live, Book Two*, 69.

exclude me from his people. "And let not any eunuch complain, "I am only a dry tree."For this is what the LORD says: "To the eunuchs who keep my Sabbaths, who choose what pleases me and hold fast to my covenant - to them I will give within my temple and its walls a memorial and a name better than sons and daughters; I will give them an everlasting name that will not be cut off.

> **HEM-** I am sought of them that asked not for (The lost-found members of the Black Nation are the ones who never sought after Allah, because they did not know how. The enemy did not teach them how to seek Allah, since they did not obey Allah, themselves); I am found to them who sought me not: I said, Behold me, behold me, unto a nation that was not called by my name. I have spread out my hands all the day unto a rebellious people, which walketh in a way that was not good (This is referring to Israel, to whom God sent prophet after prophet, to guide them into the right way, who rebelled against right guidance and then made a religion called Christianity, after their way of thinking, and put the name of Jesus on that religion to make us drink down the falsity they added to Jesus' teachings), after their own thoughts; a people that provoketh me to anger continually to my face; that sacrificeth in gardens, and burneth incense upon altars of brick (they barbecue the hog upon bricks and call it their barbecue stand); which remain among the graves (the graves mean their homes),... which eat the swine's flesh, and broth of the abominable things is in their vessels (this is referring to hog or swine in their vessels); which say, stand by thyself (This is referring to the Muslims, when it says stand by thyself), come not mean only Israel or the white race, but the white race has made the so-called Negro follow his religion,

say the same and especially those who claim sanctification in Christianity.)[113]

**HEM-** Will you turn down a Great Name which will Live Forever, Bible Is. 56:5, in exchange for the nicknames of your very enemies? They have no meaning as to a human being, such as Mr. Fish. We are human beings and should not be called Mr. Fish. They name you Mr. Hog. You are not a Hog. They call you Mr. Bird. We should not be called bird. We are not winged fowl. They are names which are worthless to human beings. The only white people who are allowed to use One of the Names of Allah (God) is one who has accepted Islam. These Names are given to them because of their faith in the religion of Allah (God). However, this does not mean that by nature these Names belong to them. It is only you, Black Brother, that by nature should be called by the Names of your God and Father, the Creator of the Heavens and the Earth. This is what Allah has taught me. Believe it or let it alone![114]

**Isaiah 58:4 KJV-** Behold, ye fast for strife and debate, and to smite with the fist of wickedness: ye shall not fast as ye do this day, to make your voice to be heard on high.

**Isaiah 58:4 NIV-** Your fasting ends in quarreling and strife, and in striking each other with wicked fists. You cannot fast as you do today and expect your voice to be heard on high.

---

[113] Muhammad, *How to Eat to Live I*, 99-100.
[114] Muhammad, *Our Saviour Has Arrived*, 102.

> **HEM-** When fasting is practiced for good, good results will follow. But if we fast, as the Bible mentions in Isaiah [58:4], just for debate, our fast is no good. The Bible teaches that the facts of people who go out and tell others that 'I had a dream' and then call dreams, visions, are not accepted. Some people tell stories about something they accomplish on the fast that they did not accomplish. The Bible answers such a person in these words: If you dream a dream, tell a dream and do not try to tell a dream for a vision from the Lord, when you did not get such a vision.[115]

**Isaiah 59:14 KJV-** And judgment is turned away backward, and justice standeth afar off: for truth is fallen in the street, and equity cannot enter.

**Isaiah 59:14 NIV-** So justice is driven back, and righteousness stands at a distance; truth has stumbled in the streets, honesty cannot enter.

> **HEM-** Again the Bible teaches us, Is. 59:14 and justice standeth afar off: for truth is fallen in the street.'[116]

**Isaiah 59:15 KJV-** Yea, truth faileth; and he that departeth from evil maketh himself a prey: and the LORD saw it, and it displeased him that there was no judgment.

**Isaiah 59:15 NIV-** Truth is nowhere to be found, and whoever shuns evil becomes a prey. The LORD looked and was displeased that there was no justice.

---

[115] Muhammad, *How to Eat to Live, Book Two*, 46-47
[116] Muhammad, Our Saviour Has Arrived, 206. See 62 for the entire revelation on the verses.

**HEM-** The greatest racists that have ever lived on our Planet Earth are the white people. We only ask for the privilege of being ourselves, seeking to restore brotherly love and respect among our people who have been divided, robbed and spoiled by the American whites. Judge Duffy has now openly spoken his hatred for any justice coming to us who have turned to do righteousness, which is the fulfillment of the prophecy which reads: "Ye, truth faileth; and judgement is turned away backward and justice standeth afar off [for the so-called Negroes] for truth is fallen in the streets and equity cannot enter. He that departed from evil maketh himself a prey: and the Lord {Master Fard Muhammad] saw it and it displeased Him that there was no judgment [justice]" (Isa. 59:15). Blessed are the so-called Negroes that depart from the evil and filthy doings of this American white man. How happy they are who seek refuge in Allah and are believers. [117]

**Isaiah 60:1-2 KJV-** Arise, shine; for thy light is come, and the glory of the LORD is risen upon thee. For, behold, the darkness shall cover the earth, and gross darkness the people: but the LORD shall arise upon thee, and his glory shall be seen upon thee.

**Isaiah 60:1-2 NIV-** Arise, shine, for your light has come, and the glory of the LORD rises upon you. See, darkness covers the earth and thick darkness is over the peoples, but the LORD rises upon you and his glory appears over you.

---

[117] Muhammad, *Message to the Blackman*, 324.

> **HEM-** The light of Truth has come to us in the Person of Master Fard Muhammad, God in Person, to Whom Praises are due forever. It is prophesied in the Bible, Is. 60:1-2, "Arise and shine, for the light has come." This is the first time that the Light of truth, the knowledge of self, and the knowledge of the enemy of self, and God, Has Been Made Manifest. This is also the first manifestation of the cause of the spiritual darkness that we have lived in for the past six thousand (6,000) years.[118]

**Isaiah 65:15 KJV-** And ye shall leave your name for a curse unto my chosen: for the Lord GOD shall slay thee, and call his servants by another name.

**Isaiah 65:15 NIV-** You will leave your name to my chosen ones as a curse; the Sovereign LORD will put you to death, but to his servants he will give another name.

> **HEM-** This is the Judgment of this world of the white race. They are bringing themselves into the Judgment of God, Himself, by trying to take vengeance, in the Last Days, on the Apostle of Truth and on his followers. Remember these words, (Bible, Is. 65:15) The Lord God shall slay thee (the enemies) and call you (who submit to His Will) by another Name.' Glory not in the name of Satan, but Glory in the Name of the Lord God of Truth Whose Name abideth forever, and His Names have the Most Beautiful Meaning. Now Allah, The God Of Islam, Invites us to accept Islam.[119]

---

[118] Muhammad, *Our Saviour Has Arrived*, 142.
[119] Ibid., 91.

**HEM-** Since the white race is more guilty than anyone else of breaking the law of Allah (God), he threatens with chastisement and total destruction. We may quote Isaiah 65:15. It reads like this: 'And ye shall leave your name for a curse unto my chosen: for the Lord God shall slay thee (the disobedient white race), and call his servants by another name. Here, we are warned that God will not accept us in the name of the white race, because He has another name that He will call us by, and He mentions this throughout Isaiah and the New Testament. We must have a name of God and not the name of an enemy of God.[120]

**Isaiah 65:17-18 KJV-** They that sanctify themselves, and purify themselves in the gardens behind one tree in the midst, eating swine's flesh, and the abomination, and the mouse, shall be consumed together, saith the LORD. For I know their works and their thoughts: it shall come, that I will gather all nations and tongues; and they shall come, and see my glory.

**Isaiah 65:17-18 NIV-** Those who consecrate and purify themselves to go into the gardens, following the one in the midst of those who eat the flesh of pigs and rats and other abominable things—they will meet their end together, declares the LORD. And I, because of their actions and their imaginations, am about to come and gather all nations and tongues, and they will come and see my glory. See note for this in NIV e-bible

**Isaiah 66:22 KJV-** For as the new heavens and the new earth, which I will make, shall remain before me, saith the

---

[120] Muhammad, *How to Eat to Live I*, 99.

LORD, so shall your seed and your name remain. Revelation 21:1-

**Isaiah 66:22 NIV-** As the new heavens and the new earth that I make will endure before me, declares the LORD, so will your name and descendants endure.

> **HEM-** Go to Asia or Africa and you will hear more about the happiness of the people over what Allah has revealed to me than among the American Black people. They all know that it is the truth that they have been waiting to learn for 6000 years. Read Isaiah 65:17 and 66:22 and Revelation 21:1 of the Bible. Read the second Surah of the Holy Qur'an. The new generation will be raised up. My main mission and work, put upon me by Allah (God), in the Person of Master Fard Muhammad, to Whom Praise is due forever, is to put you on the right path so you may go for self under the guidance of Almighty God Allah in the Person of Master Fard Muhammad. He (meaning Master Fard Muhammad) will end the present conflict between the slave and his master. If they will do anything for us of good, they will be rewarded for that good act by Allah (God), Master Fard Muhammad, and they know this.[121]

> **HEM-** A new heaven and a new earth (Bible, Isaiah 65:17, 66:22). Here is the mention of a new heavens and a new earth. Some of the scholars take it literally and some take it spiritually. I say the meaning is both literal and spiritual.[122]

---

[121] Muhammad, *Our Saviour Has Arrived*, 112-113.
[122] Ibid.

**HEM-** He makes all things new. He has the Power of heaven and earth. There have been many guesses made of just what type of power will be used in the hereafter. Some guesses have come close and some have not even scratched the surface of that which will come as a new world. You are a long way off in some of the way of thinking and understanding and knowledge of what is yet to come according to what I have been taught by Allah (God) Himself, Who Came in the Person of Master Fard Muhammad, to Whom Praises are due forever. "For, behold, I create new heavens and a new earth: the former shall not be remembered, or come into mind." Bible, Is. 65:17. Here we have a prophecy that Allah (God) Will Make All Things new. "He causes things to grow into a new growth," according to the Holy Qur'an. He Would Not Be a God Who Has Power over all things if He could not Change things according to His Will. If He Could Not Make New People of an old dead people, then He Has Not the Power to Bring In New Things because reproduction is less trouble to do and does not require such a skill as it does to Make something outright new. Here it refers to both the spiritual and the physical side, but did not He Make us in the Beginning out of nothing?[123]

**HEM-** The hog is a grafted animal, so says Allah to me- grafted from rat, cat and dog. Don't question me. This is what Allah has said, believe it, or let it alone. You have witnessed that the rat is involved in the grafting of this hog in Isaiah 66:17. 'They that sanctify themselves (self-claiming righteous of the Christians), and purify themselves in the gardens behind one tree in the midst, eating swine's flesh, and the abomination,

---

[123] Muhammad, *Our Saviour Has Arrived*, 127-128.

and the mouse, shall be consumed together, saith the Lord.' He will kill them. He doesn't want them willfully and knowingly eating such flesh, which is filled with poison in the shape of worms (trichina or pork worm) which gradually destroy humans as termites destroy timber. This filthy, evil worm can stand a temperature higher than any known flesh worm. He can't be seen with the naked eyes. You have to get the microscope. Put a little piece of his flesh (fat part), or just grease a glass slide of the microscope with his flesh. Take a look, and you will see him crawling around.[124]

**HEM-** Isaiah 66:17 condemns the people who think it is all right to eat the swine, just because white people eat it, and they think they can be holy in presence of God, or in a religion they call Christianity (which they received and have been taught is a God-verified religion). This is wrong. God never verified Christianity as being His religion. If He did, He changed His mind when He taught the prophets to submit to Him. The Arabic word for this is Islam, which means to submit.[125]

**HEM-** Christians are among the largest consumers of pork in America, and they deliver this rat throughout the world to other people. They are so fond of swine flesh that they sacrifice it in the church, and then ask divine blessing upon it. They barbecue and cook it, and hold a feast in their places of worship and eat this slow death poisonous animal which God has forbidden as though they had an option with God. No wonder Isaiah says that they stand behind one tree in the

---

[124] Muhammad, *How to Eat to Live I*, 70-71.
[125] Ibid., 96-97.

garden, eating swine flesh, the abomination, the mouse and the broth of the swine in their vessels. And yet, they will tell all the Muslims and Orthodox Jews that they are holier than we who don't dare even to touch the swine's carcass.[126]

There are so many little new groups that call themselves sanctified, holy, Jesusified, Christified, and Godified. Such people should read this chapter, Isaiah 66:17-18. "They that sanctify themselves , and purify themselves in the gardens behind one tree in the midst, eating swine's flesh, and the abomination, and the mouse, shall be consumed together, saith the Lord." Death is for you who eat the swine. God will not accept swine eaters as His people, after knowledge that the swine is a divinely-prohibited flesh. The hog (swine), God has taught me, in the Person of Master Fard Muhammad, To Whom praise is due forever, was made from the grafting of cat and dog. The rat is mentioned in the above quoted verse of Isaiah, but the cat and dog are not mentioned. The white theologians knew that if they had given the names of these two animals (the cat and the dog), you would have probably not accepted the hog. But, Who is better knowing than Allah.[127]

**HEM-** See Isaiah 66:18: "For I know their works and their thoughts: it shall come, that I will gather all nations and tongues; and they shall come, and see my glory." The glory means the right way that He will teach the people in the last days; that He will approve of our doing what He gives to us in the Resurrection. He knows your works that ignore His law of

---

[126] Muhammad, *How to Eat to Live I*, 13.
[127] Ibid., 97.

righteousness, given to His prophets of old, and your self-centered thoughts, or your thinking that you can deceive others, while breaking the law of God, into thinking you are right in eating the swine. But, He has promised death to you in the 17th verse. He will consume such people all together.[128]

**HEM-** We must remember that these warnings given in the 17th and 18th verses of Isaiah are referring to the general resurrection, and the accountability of our actions and disobedience to the law of God, because the 18th verse says, "...it shall come that I will gather all nations and tongues." This is also prophesied in Matthew 25:32: "And before him shall be gathered all nations..."[129]

**HEM-** They glorify the eating of the hog as though God is with them to eat what He has made a curse, as Isaiah mentioned it, they called themselves in eating hog (66:17). Now here comes the Muslims who have been the slaves of Christian America, wanting to obey the Bible, but they are tried by force to not obey the Bible. The Brotherhood of the Muslims is what Paul and his Epistles preached; the Brotherhood gets to clear sunshine.[130]

**HEM-** Also in the Bible Isaiah mentioned the long life of the righteous in these worlds: "that a person one hundred (100) years old will be like a child"...meaning that their age will never cause them to look old. They will have the freshness of youth says the prophet, Isaiah. And the Holy Qur'an, also verifies the same.

---

[128] Muhammad, *How to Eat to Live I*, 98-99.
[129] Ibid., 99.
[130] Muhammad, *How to Eat to Live II*, 121-122.

Allah (God) in the Person of Master Fard Muhammad, to Whom Praises are Due forever -- out of His Own Mouth -- Said to me that He Causes us to Grow into a New Growth. And that we would have the look and the energy of one who is sixteen (16) years of age and our youth and energy of a sixteen year-old would last forever.[131]

---

[131] Muhammad, *Our Saviour Has Arrived*, 114.

# Chapter XIII:

## Jeremiah

**Jeremiah 2:14 KJV-** Is Israel a servant? Is he a home born slave? Why is he spoiled?

**Jeremiah 2:14 NIV-** Is Israel a servant, a slave by birth? Why then has he become plunder?

> **HEM-** With the fight going on in the South between the slaves and their masters, the slaves (in mind) have become home-born slaves as it is written (Jer. 2:14). They love their master and desire to be their master's kin in the line of true brotherhood. This is the truth which cannot be hidden in these modern times. The intelligent people and the college university graduates are poisoned 100 per cent more in mind and into the love of the enemy than the uneducated. It is no wonder that the scriptures say the poor gladly receive the truth as being offered heaven at once from Almighty Allah (God) Himself.[132]

**Jeremiah 49:21 KJV-** The earth is moved at the noise of their fall, at the cry the noise thereof was heard in the Red sea.

**Jeremiah 49:21 NIV-** At the sound of their fall the earth will tremble; their cry will resound to the Red Sea.

> **HEM-** The white race was given a limited time (6,000 years) to be overlord (white) of our earth and

---
[132] Muhammad, *Message to the Blackman in America*, 232.

ourselves. He is well aware of it (time). The white man is well aware that he does not own the earth and that he had no part in its creation. The scientists of the white race well know this, but, nevertheless, as it is written (Bible) Jer. 49:21, we see that today trouble is brewing everywhere; even between Black and Black where it should not be. But where Black wants to live with white and does not want to take his responsibility to go for self, Black has trouble with Black due to this desire. Integration is against the Desire and Will of God Who Wants and must Do that which is written He Will Come and Do: Restore the earth to its rightful owner (Black Man).[133]

**Jeremiah 50:6-7 KJV-** My people hath been lost sheep: their shepherds have caused them to go astray; they have turned them away on the mountains: they have gone from mountain to hill, they have forgotten their resting place. All that found them have devoured them: and their adversaries said, We offend not, because they have sinned against the LORD, the habitation of justice, even the LORD, the hope of their fathers.

**Jeremiah 50:6-7 NIV-** My people have been lost sheep; their shepherds have led them astray and caused them to roam on the mountains. They wandered over mountain and hill and forgot their own resting place. Whoever found them devoured them; their enemies said, 'We are not guilty, for they sinned against the LORD, their true pasture, the LORD, the hope of their fathers.'

---

[133] Muhammad, *Our Saviour Has Arrive*,104.

> **HEM-** Jer. 50:6- "My people hath been lost sheep: their shepherds have caused them to go astray, they (white and Black preachers of Christianity) have turned them away on the mountains: they have gone from mountain to hill, they have forgotten their resting place." (Their native people and country). Jer. 50:7 " All that found them have devoured them: and their adversaries said, We offend not, because they have sinned against the Lord, the habitation of justice, even the Lord, the hope of their fathers." Since the white man has made the so-called Negro as wicked a person as himself now, these are the words that he speaks: "They are just as evil as we; therefore, Allah God is against them, too." The so-called Negro repeats the same and says the white man is no worse than the so-called Negro.[134]

**Jeremiah 50:24 KJV-** I have laid a snare for thee, and thou art also taken, O Babylon, and thou wast not aware: thou art found, and also caught, because thou hast striven against the LORD.

**Jeremiah 50:24 NIV-** I set a trap for you, O Babylon, and you were caught before you knew it; you were found and captured because you opposed the LORD.

> **HEM-** Go to sleep to the reality of the judgment of America, a repetition of ancient Babylon's judgment, if you like to be caught in the snare. As God has said, He laid a snare for ancient Babylon (Jeremiah 50:24) and ancient Babylon was taken in that snare. So it is in America. Long before America ever thought that she should repent of her evil done to her slaves or reject

---

[134] Muhammad, *The Fall of America*, 197.

repentance, God hath set the snare to catch her. America is now in the same snare that God set for ancient Babylon. Will America repent that she should be healed or will she ignore it?[135]

**Jeremiah 50:46 KJV-** At the noise of the taking of Babylon the earth is moved, and the cry is heard among the nations.

**Jeremiah 50:46 NIV-** At the sound of Babylon's capture the earth will tremble; its cry will resound among the nations.

> **HEM-** In The Fall of Ancient Babylon Jer. 50:46, "At the noise of the taking of Babylon the earth is moved, and the cry is heard among the nations." here the Bible teaches us and we see today, at the fall of the old world, there is a great noise of war, the fighting of war, the destruction of nations, towns, and cities and the killing of their citizens. There is disagreement and confusion of the head of nations.[136]

> **HEM-** Come Follow Me, I say. I will lead you to your God of Salvation. If you stay where you are, you will suffer the consequences. Just as a reminder, read the Bible Jer. 50:46 and II Pet. 3:10. It is terrible, awful, and frightful; to look up and instead of seeing a blue sky, see a sky of flames and fire. This will surely come. Allah (God) has affirmed this prophecy with me. The whole heavens will be blotted out and in its place there will be a canopy of flame. The heavens and elements that make up the atmosphere of the earth will melt with fervent heat. There will be an explosion of the total atmosphere of the earth by God Himself. Take

---

[135] Muhammad, *The Fall of America*, 137.
[136] Ibid., 212-213

Heed of it, for the Holy Qur'an says such a time as we are entering into now is a grievous time. It will make children's hair turn gray. If the grief and excitement will make children turn gray because of the terribleness of judgment, what do you think our hair will be doing? The Bible prophesies gray and baldness upon all heads.[137]

**Jeremiah 50:31 KJV-** Behold, I am against thee, O thou most proud, saith the Lord GOD of hosts: for thy day is come, the time that I will visit thee.

**Jeremiah 50:31 KJV-** See, I am against you, O arrogant one," declares the Lord, the LORD Almighty, "for your day has come, the time for you to be punished.

> **HEM-** Jer. 50:31 prophesies: "Behold, I am against thee, O thou most proud, saith the Lord God of hosts: for thy day is come, the time that I will visit thee." Allah (God) is visiting America with great destruction which He has to pour upon wicked America. After their mistreatment of the so-called Negro for four hundred years, she desires now to deceive them and to cause them to suffer with her and share in her doom.[138]

**Jeremiah 51:1 KJV-** Thus saith the LORD; Behold, I will raise up against Babylon, and against them that dwell in the midst of them that rise up against me, a destroying wind.

---

[137] Muhammad, *The Fall of America*, 105-106
[138] Ibid., 196-97.

**Jeremiah 51:1 NIV-** This is what the LORD says: "See, I will stir up the spirit of a destroyer against Babylon and the people of Leb Kamai.

> **HEM-** The Bible mentions that God used a destroying wind (Jeremiah 51:1) against those who opposed His purpose and aims. Is it not true that day and night somewhere in America there are destructive tornadoes and storms destroying the property and lives of Americans?[139]

**Jeremiah 51:8 KJV-** Babylon is suddenly fallen and destroyed: howl for her; take balm for her pain, if so be she may be healed.

**Jeremiah 51:8 NIV-** Babylon will suddenly fall and be broken. Wail over her! Get balm for her pain; perhaps she can be healed.

> **HEM-** America compared with Babylon 51:8- I compare the fall of America with the fall of ancient Babylon. Her wickedness (sins), is the same as history shows of ancient Babylon. "Babylon is suddenly fallen and the destroyed howl for her; take balm for her pains, if so she may be healed." What were the sins of ancient Babylon? According to history she was rich; she was proud and her riches increased her corruption. She had every merchandise that the nations wanted or demanded; her ships carried her merchandise to the ports of every nation. She was a drunkard; wine and strong drinks were in her daily practice. She was filled with adultery and murder; she persecuted and killed

---

[139] Muhammad, *The Fall of America*, 137

the people of God. She killed the saints and prophets of Allah (God). Hate and filthiness, gambling, sports of every evil as you practice in America were practiced in Babylon. Only America is modern and much worse. Ancient Babylon was destroyed by her neighboring nations.[140]

**Jeremiah 51:9 KJV-** We would have healed Babylon, but she is not healed: forsake her, and let us go every one into his own country: for her judgment reacheth unto heaven, and is lifted up even to the skies.

**Jeremiah 51:9 NIV-** We would have healed Babylon, but she cannot be healed; let us leave her and each go to his own land, for her judgment reaches to the skies, it rises as high as the clouds.

> **HEM-** America seems to be the answer to many of the Bible's and the Holy Qur'an's prophecies. It is mentioned in Jeremiah (51:9) that ancient Babylon could have been healed but was not, for her wickedness was such that she was neither healed nor forgiven. The charges against ancient Babylon, according to her history, were that she persecuted and imprisoned the Jews. She brought them into captivity from Jerusalem after the taking of Jerusalem by Nebuchadnezzar.[141]
>
> **HEM-** The most dreadful divine judgments that have ever been witnessed by man are now coming on

---

[140] Muhammad, *Message to the Blackman*, 273. In this publication of **Message to the Blackman in America** and others Jer. 51:8 is written as Jer. 51:81. This is an error in the publication and appears here as the Honorable Elijah Muhammad referenced it (Jer. 51:8). It should be noted that Jeremiah only has 64 verses in chapter 51.

[141] Muhammad, *The Fall of America*, 130.

America. America is the divine target because she could have bettered herself in the divine eyes of Allah (God), Who came in the Person of Master Fard Muhammad, to Whom praises are due forever. But America did not and will not better herself, as it is written and prophesied, concerning Ancient Babylon and Egypt. "We would have healed Babylon, but she is not healed:...." Bible, Je. 51:9, (because she was not willing to do justice by her captive Jews from Jerusalem).[142]

**Jeremiah 51:25 KJV-** Behold, I am against thee, O destroying mountain, saith the LORD, which destroyest all the earth: and I will stretch out mine hand upon thee, and roll thee down from the rocks, and will make thee a burnt mountain.

**Jeremiah 51:25 NIV-** I am against you, O destroying mountain, you who destroy the whole earth," declares the LORD. "I will stretch out my hand against you, roll you off the cliffs, and make you a burned-out mountain.

**HEM-** Now it is the hand of God which is after America to force her into submission -- a hand from which we have no defense as it is written and prophesied in the Bible, under the name of Babylon. Jeremiah 51:25: "Behold, I am against thee, O destroying mountain, saith the Lord, which destroyest all the earth: and I will stretch out mine hand upon thee, and roll thee down from the rocks, and will make thee a burnt mountain."[143]

---

[142] Muhammad, *The Fall of America*, 232.
[143] Ibid., 194.

**Jeremiah 51:45 KJV-** My people, go ye out of the midst of her, and deliver ye every man his soul from the fierce anger of the LORD.

**Jeremiah 51:45 NIV-** Come out of her, my people! Run for your lives! Run from the fierce anger of the LORD.

> **HEM-** Jeremiah (51:45) mentions a warning to the people of God to flee out of Babylon. Could this be referring to the captive Jews in ancient Babylon? If God called the ancient Jews His people, it was for a sign of a future people that He would choose to call His people (The American so-called Negro).[144]
>
> **HEM-** In ancient Babylon's history, the enslaved Jews were ordered to flee out of her midst and be delivered, every man his soul from the fierce anger of the Lord, Jeremiah (51:45).[145]
>
> **HEM-** This showed that God was going to plague Babylon; and that His people should not suffer the divine plagues sent upon Babylon. They are ordered to flee out of her. (Jeremiah 51:45.) This is a future prophecy of a future Babylon similar to the ancient Babylon under the rule of Nebuchadnezzar. The history of these two kings of ancient Babylon teaches us that they held slaves who were trying to serve the right God.[146]
>
> **HEM-** America now is at war with God through God's people (the so-called Negro.) The confusion and the

---

[144] Muhammad, *The Fall of America*, 133.
[145] Ibid.
[146] Ibid., 134.

plagues of the country with disasters, one after another, is divine retaliation against white America's evil doings and intentions, against her once-slaves and her false friendship, which has her opening her homes to integrate the people of God with them who by nature are different or foreign. The white man has poisoned our people's minds so thoroughly that they fight against their own God and salvation to gain the favor of their own enemies. The call of Islam, the true religion of God to us, the once-slaves of America, is the same call telling us to flee out of the American way of life so that our lives may be saved from the divine destruction of a non-repentant enemy (Jeremiah 51:45.)[147]

**HEM-** The white man has opened all of his doors and avenues of temptation to lure the Negro in for total destruction. Again we have a warning to leave a people with whom God is angry as the people of ancient Babylon were warned to do. Jer. 51:45 -- "My people, go yet out of the midst of her, and deliver ye every man his soul from the fierce anger of the Lord." All of the plagues, destructions and judgment which Allah (God) used to destroy the wicked and disobedient from the time of Adam until this day will be brought upon America. Then she will be burned with fire. This is the time of trouble that shall bring America into insanity.[148]

**Jeremiah 51:46-47 KJV-** And lest your heart faint, and ye fear for the rumour that shall be heard in the land; a rumour shall both come one year, and after that in another

---

[147] Muhammad, *The Fall of America*, 135.
[148] Ibid., 197-98.

year shall come a rumour, and violence in the land, ruler against ruler. Therefore, behold, the days come, that I will do judgment upon the graven images of Babylon: and her whole land shall be confounded, and all her slain shall fall in the midst of her.

**Jeremiah 51:46-47 NIV-** Do not lose heart or be afraid when rumors are heard in the land; one rumor comes this year, another the next, rumors of violence in the land and of ruler against ruler. For the time will surely come when I will punish the idols of Babylon; her whole land will be disgraced and her slain will all lie fallen within her.

> **HEM-** Jeremiah (51:46) prophesies violence in the midst of Babylon (a future Babylon) and "ruler against ruler." Is not this true of the American government and people today? "Her whole land (people) shall be confounded" (Jeremiah 51:47.) Is not this true of the American government and people today? They are fast becoming confounded. "And all her slain shall fall in the midst of her" (Jeremiah 51:47.) Every hour in the day and night people are being murdered and killed in America throughout her cities and highways. Murdering and killing is the order of the day in America.[149]

**Jeremiah 51:53 KJV-** Though Babylon should mount up to heaven, and though she should fortify the height of her strength, yet from me shall spoilers come unto her, saith the LORD.

---

[149] Muhammad, *The Fall of America*, 136-37.

**Jeremiah 51:53 NIV-** Even if Babylon reaches the sky and fortifies her lofty stronghold, I will send destroyers against her," declares the LORD.

**HEM-** Jer. 51:53 says: "Though Babylon should mount up to heaven, and though she should fortify the height of her strength, yet from me shall spoilers come unto her saith the Lord. America is under a destruction similar to that of ancient Babylon. In the Bible, Jeremiah, Isaiah, and Revelation of John prophesied concerning her. Babylon, there-mentioned is a future Babylon, and not a Babylon of the past.[150]

---

[150] Muhammad, *The Fall of America*, 194.

# Chapter XIV:

## Ezekiel

**HEM-** Hundreds and thousands of preachers tremble at the thought of even accepting the truth, and wish to take their followers into the "Fall of America." This is the problem to be solved. If it is to be solved then how shall it be solved: and what is the best method to use in the solution? It must be a solution that touches, not only the enemy, but those who cleave to him while defying the wrath of Almighty Allah (God). It is incumbent (says the Holy Quran) that Allah give life to this mentally dead so-called Negro.

It is also made incumbent in the Bible where Ezekiel declares (in his vision) that all of the dry bones were resurrected. This does not refer so much to the word because the word has no effect on their resurrection. It literally took something more effective than the word. The winds that the prophets were to prophesy to represent wars which will eventually bring harm and suffering to the rebellious rejecters of the truth. Salvation must come to the so-called Negro. Everyone's eyes should be opened. The time of the ending of this world is now, and not yet to come, as you so foolishly thinks.[151]

**Ezekiel 1:16 KJV-** The appearance of the wheels and their work was like unto the colour of a beryl: and they four had one likeness: and their appearance and their work was as it were a wheel in the middle of a wheel.

---

[151] Muhammad, *The Fall of America*, 19.

**Ezekiel 1:16 KJV-** This was the appearance and structure of the wheels: They sparkled like chrysolite, and all four looked alike. Each appeared to be made like a wheel intersecting a wheel.

> **HEM-** Ezekiel saw the Mother Plane in a vision. According to the Bible, he looked up and saw this Plane (Ez. 1:16) and he called it a wheel because it was made like a wheel. A Plane that is wheel-shaped can turn in any direction, at any time. He admitted that the Plane was so high that it looked dreadful, and he cried out, "O wheel" (Ez. 10:13). Ezekiel saw great work going on in the wheel and four living creatures "and their work was as it were a wheel in the middle of a wheel." (Ez. 1:16). And when the living creatures went, the wheels went with them: and when the living creatures were lifted up from the earth, the wheels were lifted up Ez. 1:19. The power of the lifting up of the four creatures was in the wheel.[152]

**Ezekiel 1:19 KJV-** And when the living creatures went, the wheels went by them: and when the living creatures were lifted up from the earth, the wheels were lifted up.

**Ezekiel 1:19 NIV-** When the living creatures moved, the wheels beside them moved; and when the living creatures rose from the ground, the wheels also rose. [153]

**Ezekiel 10:13 KJV-** As for the wheels, it was cried unto them in my hearing, O wheel.

---

[152] Muhammad, *The Fall of America*, 238.
[153] See The Hon. Elijah Muhammad's revelation associated with Ezekiel 1:16.

**Ezekiel 10:13 KJV-** I heard the wheels being called "the whirling wheels." [154]

**Ezekiel 7:25 KJV-** Destruction cometh; and they shall seek peace, and there shall be none.

**Ezekiel 7:25 NIV-** When terror comes, they will seek peace, but there will be none.

> **HEM-** Christianity now seeks peace but she is guilty of making trouble and of starting the woes that the people now suffer. She seeks peace and seems not to be able to find it. She runs to and fro, to nations, capitols of nations, leaders and rulers, seeking peace, but finds none, it is clear, as it is written, Bible, Ez. 7:25.[155]

**Ezekiel 14:13 KJV-** Son of man, when the land sinneth against me by trespassing grievously, then will I stretch out mine hand upon it, and will break the staff of the bread thereof, and will send famine upon it, and will cut off man and beast from it.

**Ezekiel 14:13 NIV-** Son of man, if a country sins against me by being unfaithful and I stretch out my hand against it to cut off its food supply and send famine upon it and kill its men and their animals.

> **HEM-** I warn you to let their (Babylon) destruction serve as a warning for America. This people has gone to the limit in doing evil; as God dealt with ancient

---

[154] See Ezekiel 1:16.
[155] Muhammad, *Our Saviour Has Arrived*, 204.

people, so he will deal with the modern Babylon (America). As God says: "Son of Man, when the land (people) sinneth against Me by trespassing grievously, then will I stretch out Mine hand upon it, and will break the staff of bread thereof, and will send famine upon it, and will cut off man and beast from it."[156]

**Ezekiel 18:31KJV-** Cast away from you all your transgressions, whereby ye have transgressed; and make you a new heart and a new spirit: for why will ye die, O house of Israel?

**Ezekiel 18:31NIV-** Rid yourselves of all the offenses you have committed, and get a new heart and a new spirit. Why will you die, O house of Israel?

> **HEM-** As the God of Truth, Justice, and Righteousness, Allah Is Going to Be the Ruler or the Creator of the New Government. Then by no means can He carry any of the old world into His New kingdom of Truth, Justice, Equality, and Peace. We must have a new government and a new people to operate the new government (Bible Ez. 18:31).[157]

> **HEM-** After the destruction of the old world by fire and by other means of destruction, there is nothing of the old wicked world that can be salvaged to carry into the new world of righteousness. Note Bible, Ez.18:31.[158]

**Ezekiel 21:7 KJV-** And it shall be, when they say unto thee, Wherefore sighest thou? that thou shalt answer, For

---

[156] Muhammad, *Message to the Blackman*, 273.
[157] Muhammad, *Our Saviour Has Arrived*, 113.
[158] Ibid.

the tidings; because it cometh: and every heart shall melt, and all hands shall be feeble, and every spirit shall faint, and all knees shall be weak as water: behold, it cometh, and shall be brought to pass, saith the Lord GOD.

**Ezekiel 21:7 NIV-** And when they ask you, 'Why are you groaning?' you shall say, 'Because of the news that is coming. Every heart will melt and every hand go limp; every spirit will become faint and every knee become as weak as water.' It is coming! It will surely take place, declares the Sovereign LORD.

**Ezekiel 21:15 KJV-** I have set the point of the sword against all their gates, that their heart may faint, and their ruins be multiplied: ah! it is made bright, it is wrapped up for the slaughter.

**Ezekiel 21:15 NIV-** So that hearts may melt and the fallen be many, I have stationed the sword for slaughter at all their gates. Oh! It is made to flash like lightning, it is grasped for slaughter.

> **HEM-** You [the devil] have boasted that you could police the world and have come pretty near doing so but have failed to the 'Bear' behind the tree and the 'Lion' in the thicket. The sky over you is being filled with your enemy's arms which can be seen with the naked eye. Your scientists are troubled and at their wits' end to find time to make ready, as it is written: 'I have set the point of the sword against all their gates; that their heart may faint, and their ruins be multiplied. Ah! it is made bright, it is wrapped up for the slaughter' (Ez.21:15). Answer: "For the tidings;

because it cometh and every heart shall melt, and all hands shall be feeble and every spirit shall faint, and all knees shall be weak as water."(Ezekiel 21:7)[159]

## Ezekiel 34 KJV-

**HEM-** As Jesus was not of the world of the white man, so are we of the world of the white man. And the parable that he put before you prophesies how God would come, searching for you to take you out of the world of the wicked, and put you into your own world of Peace and security. Also see Bible (Ez. 34 Bible).[160]

**Ezekiel 36:24 KJV-** For I will take you from among the nations, gather you out of all countries, and bring you into your own land.

**Ezekiel 36:24 NIV-** For I will take you out of the nations; I will gather you from all the countries and bring you back into your own land.

**HEM-** The time is now ripe that they should have no fear, only the fear of Allah, Who is in person among them to save them from their enemies. By all means, they must be separated from the white race, in order that the scripture might be fulfilled. "For I will take you from among the heathen and gather you out of all countries and will bring you into your own land." [161]

**Ezekiel 47:12 KJV-** Along the bank of the river, on this side and that, will grow all kinds of trees used for food;

---

[159] Muhammad, *Message to the Blackman*, 299-300.
[160] Muhammad, *Our Saviour Has Arrived*, 194.
[161] Muhammad, *Message to the Blackman in America*, 20.

their leaves will not wither, and their fruit will not fail. They will bear fruit every month, because their water flows from the sanctuary. Their fruit will be for food, and their leaves for medicine.

**Ezekiel 47:12 NIV-** Fruit trees of all kinds will grow on both banks of the river. Their leaves will not wither, nor will their fruit fail. Every month they will bear, because the water from the sanctuary flows to them. Their fruit will serve for food and their leaves for healing.

> **HEM-** The prophet (Eze. 47:12, Bible) says that Allah (God) will even make new trees and shall bring forth new fruit. Jn. 13:34 prophesies that a new commandment shall be given to us which will make you able ministers of a new testament. 2 Cor. 3:6 and 2 Cor. 5:17 says that "if any man be in Christ, he is a new creature." Eph. 2:15, prophesies "of twain, one new man, so making peace." The Bible, 2 Pet. 3:13, prophesies, "We look for new heaven and a new earth" and Rev. 21:5, "He said, behold, I make all things new." Since the Bible here has promised through the mouth of the prophets that Allah (God) Raised Up in Israel will be brought about when the God of the Resurrection of the Dead Appears, the Dead will no more be as they once were. They will become new creatures.[162]

---

[162] Muhammad, *Our Saviour Has Arrived*, 114.

# Chapter XV:

# Daniel

**HEM-** Study your own Bible (it is there.) The end is predicted and hinted in many places. Daniel (in the Bible) however gives you a better knowledge of it than in any other place. And the Quran prophecy is exact. Do not expect ten more years; the fall will be within a few days. The so-called Negro must be stripped completely of the white man's way of life, his name and Christianity. The world of scholars and scientists knows that Christianity will not survive. They know Islam is the only religion that will survive the destruction of this wicked civilization.[163]

**HEM-** I thank Allah in the Person of Master Fard Muhammad, to Whom praise is due forever, who has come to deliver the Black man in America and to kill our oppressors. This is very good, and we should be shouting day and night that a deliverer has come. The revelation of the Bible has given this people the right name (a beast) and a most vicious description does the revelation give. In Daniel of the Bible, this people are described as a beast rising up out of the sea with three ribs of a man in its mouth. This is the description of America with the Black slaves swallowed for three centuries in the power of our enemies (the devils).[164]

**HEM-** Allah (God) has come to take over and to guide another people into setting up a better educational system for the people of whom He Himself is the

---

[163] Muhammad, *The Fall of America*, 19.
[164] Ibid., 81.

Head. And we all get guidance from Him, as Daniel said in his prophesy, "God will set up a kingdom and He will leave it into the hands of others, but He Himself will guide it." But first He must remove all the rubbish if this white man's world educational system. He discards America's educational system, as we discard rubbish to be burned up.[165]

## Daniel (Chapter 4)

**HEM-** Let us look again at our own Black independence and how it came on this same day of the 4th of July....at the Coming of Allah (God) Who came in the Person of Master Fard Muhammad, to Whom praises are due forever, on July 4, 1930. The significance of His coming to us, on the Independence Day of the white man, is very great. It is their day of great rejoicing. As with former peoples and their governments, their destruction took place when they were at the height of their rejoicing. Nebuchadnezzar, according to the Bible history of him, (Dan. Ch.4) was walking around in his palace and proudly looking around and admiring the skill of the work he had set up and said, "Has not all this my hand wrought?" The Bible teaches us that while the words were in his mouth, the end came. Allah (God) changed his mind and heart from that of a civilized man to the mind and heart of a beast. He had the brain reactions of a wild beast and he was cast out among the dumb brutes.[166]

**Daniel 7:9 KJV-** I beheld till the thrones were cast down, and the Ancient of days did sit, whose garment was white

---

[165] Muhammad, *The Fall of America*, 93.
[166] Ibid., 68-69.

as snow, and the hair of his head like the pure wool: his throne was like the fiery flame and his wheels as burning fire.

**Daniel 7:9 NIV-** As I looked, thrones were set in place, and the Ancient of Days took his seat. His clothing was as white as snow; the hair of his head was white like wool. His throne was flaming with fire, and its wheels were all ablaze.

> **HEM-** We must do our utmost to keep our nation pure by keeping the white race away from our women. We're proud of our Black skin and our kinky wool; for this kinky wool hair is that of the future ruler. Look into your poison book, Dan. 7:9, Rev. 1:14. It has been boasted that America is a white man's country, but why did they bring us here? If the white race is such a super race, why don't they live alone and leave us to live alone in our own country? Why are they fighting to stay in Asia? Why not be satisfied with Europe and America? We didn't ask to be brought here.[167]

**Daniel 7:11,19 KJV-** **11** I beheld then because of the voice of the great words which the horn spake: I beheld even till the beast was slain, and his body destroyed, and given to the burning flame. **19** Then I would know the truth of the fourth beast, which was diverse from all the others, exceeding dreadful, whose teeth were of iron, and his nails of brass; which devoured, brake in pieces, and stamped the residue with his feet.

---

[167] Muhammad, *Our Saviour Has Arrived*, 87.

**Daniel 7:11, 19 NIV- 11** Then I continued to watch because of the boastful words the horn was speaking. I kept looking until the beast was slain and its body destroyed and thrown into the blazing fire. **19** Then I wanted to know the true meaning of the fourth beast, which was different from all the others and most terrifying, with its iron teeth and bronze claws—the beast that crushed and devoured its victims and trampled underfoot whatever was left.

> **HEM-** The so-called Negroes are made so poisoned by this wicked of devils that they love them more than they love their own people. It is really because of the evil done to them by the American white race that Allah (God) has put them on His list, as the first to be destroyed. The others will be given a little longer to live, as the prophet Daniel says.[168]

**Daniel 9:26-27 KJV-** And after threescore and two weeks shall Messiah be cut off, but not for himself: and the people of the prince that shall come shall destroy the city and the sanctuary; and the end thereof shall be with a flood, and unto the end of the war desolations are determined. And he shall confirm the covenant with many for one week: and in the midst of the week he shall cause the sacrifice and the oblation to cease, and for the overspreading of abominations he shall make it desolate, even until the consummation, and that determined shall be poured upon the desolate.

**Daniel 9:26-27 NIV-** After the sixty-two 'sevens,' the Anointed One will be cut off and will have nothing. The

---

[168] Muhammad, *Message to the Blackman in America*, 88.

people of the ruler who will come will destroy the city and the sanctuary. The end will come like a flood: War will continue until the end, and desolations have been decreed. ²⁷ He will confirm a covenant with many for one 'seven.' In the middle of the 'seven' he will put an end to sacrifice and offering. And on a wing of the temple he will set up an abomination that causes desolation, until the end that is decreed is poured out on him."

> **HEM-** After the war, "and unto the end of the war, desolations are determined....and that determined shall be poured upon the desolate." (Bible Dan. 9:26-27) I want you to know that, that which will be poured means: it is the deprivation of you, America, of your ever getting back into power again to attack the nations of the earth.[169]

> **HEM-** The Son of man comes to judge man and mankind. The day, the day, the day had come! As Daniel prophesied, (Bible, Dan 9:26,27) "...and unto the end the war desolations are determined." "...and for the overspreading of abominations he shall make it desolate, even until the consummation, and that determined shall be poured upon the desolate." Just think about it! At the end of the war, desolation; so that puts an end to the hope of those who expect to see a great boost of prosperity after the war![170]

---

[169] Muhammad, *The Fall of America*, 204.
[170] Ibid., 250.

# Chapter XVI:

# Hosea

**Hosea 11:9 KJV-** I will not execute the fierceness of mine anger, I will not return to destroy Ephraim: for I am God, and not man; the Holy One in the midst of thee: and I will not enter into the city.

**Hosea 11:9 NIV-** I will not carry out my fierce anger, nor will I turn and devastate Ephraim. For I am God, and not man - the Holy One among you. I will not come in wrath.

> **HEM-** A father has pleasure in his son and in his son's affairs because his son is a part of himself and his very image and likeness. There is no true scripture that teaches us that God is something other than a man. The Bible teaches us (Hosea 11:9): 'For I am God and not man; the Holy One in the midst of thee.' Here the latter part of the verse makes it clear that God is a Holy One (man) and the man that he is not is an unholy one (man). This only means that the Holy God is not the wicked man's God (the Caucasian race).[171]

---

[171] Muhammad, *Our Saviour Has Arrived,* 66.

# Chapter XVII:

# Joel

**Joel 2:2 KJV-** A day of darkness and of gloominess, a day of clouds and of thick darkness, as the morning spread upon the mountains: a great people and a strong; there hath not been ever the like, neither shall be any more after it, even to the years of many generations.

**Joel 2:2 NIV-** A day of darkness and gloom, a day of clouds and blackness. Like dawn spreading across the mountains a large and mighty army comes, such as never was of old nor ever will be in ages to come.

> **HEM-** The years 1965-1966 are going to be fateful for America bringing in the "Fall of America". As one of the prophets of the Bible prophesied in regard to her, "As the morning spreads abroad upon the mountains a great and strong people set in battle array."[172]
>
> **HEM-** One of the prophets of the Bible prophesied in regard to America, "As the morning spreads abroad upon the mountains, a great and strong people set in battle array." (Joel 2:2). This is the setting of the nations for a showdown to determine who will live on earth. The survivor is to build a nation of peace to rule the people of the earth forever under the guidance of Almighty God, Allah. With the nations setting forth for a final war at this time, God pleads for His people (the inheritors of the earth; the so-called Negroes).[173]

---

[172] Muhammad, *Message to the Blackman in America*, 270.
[173] Muhammad, *The Fall of America*, 175-76.

**Joel 3:2-3 KJV-** I will also gather all nations, and will bring them down into the valley of Jehoshaphat, and will plead with them there for my people and for my heritage Israel, whom they have scattered among the nations, and parted my land. And they have cast lots for my people; and have given a boy for an harlot, and sold a girl for wine, that they might drink.

**Joel 3:2-3 NIV-** I will gather all nations and bring them down to the Valley of Jehoshaphat. There I will enter into judgment against them concerning my inheritance, my people Israel, for they scattered my people among the nations and divided up my land. They cast lots for my people and traded boys for prostitutes; they sold girls for wine that they might drink.

> **HEM-** It is clear that the armies of the nations of the earth have geared themselves for a showdown between their forces and Allah and the Nation of Islam. We, the so-called American Negroes, the lost and found members of our Nation, are in this decision. The second and third verses of this same chapter (Chapter 3) read like this: "I will also gather all nations and will bring them down into the valley of Jehoshaphat [Europe and Asia- between black and white] and will plead with them there for my people and for my heritage [the lost and found, so- called Negroes], Israel whom they have scattered among the nations and parted my land [between the European white race] and they have casted lots for my people and have given a boy for a harlot and sold a girl for wine that they might drink."[174]

---

[174] Muhammad, *The Fall of America*, 268.

**Joel 3:7 KJV-** Behold, I will raise them out of the place whither ye have sold them, and will return your recompense upon your own head.

**Joel 3:7 NIV-** See, I am going to rouse them out of the places to which you sold them, and I will return on your own heads what you have done.

> **HEM-** America has fulfilled this to the very letter and spirit with her slaves (the so-called Negroes) under the type of Israel. The Egyptians did nothing of the kind to Israel when they were in bondage to them. In fact, and as God taught me, the Bible is not referring to those people as His people; it is referring to the so-called Negro and his enemy (the white race). The seventh verse also gives us a hint in this way: "Behold, I will raise them out of the place where you have sold them and will return your recompense upon your own head."[175]

**Joel 3:9 KJV-** Proclaim ye this among the Gentiles; Prepare war, wake up the mighty men, let all the men of war draw near; let them come up.

**Joel 3:9 NIV-** Proclaim this among the nations: Prepare for war! Rouse the warriors! Let all the fighting men draw near and attack.

> **HEM-** "Proclaim you among the Gentiles, prepare war, wake up the mighty men, let all of the men of war

---

[175] Muhammad, *The Fall of America*, 268.

draw near, let them come up." All the mighty men of science and modern warfare have been called in an effort to devise instruments and weapons against God and the armies of heaven. The nations of the earth are angry. The disbelievers and hypocrites of my people also are angry over the change of the old world to a new world of justice and righteousness, causing much spiritual darkness and misunderstanding to fall upon them. They want to judge the person Allah should choose for His Messenger.[176]

**Joel 3:14 KJV-** Multitudes, multitudes in the valley of decision: for the day of the LORD is near in the valley of decision.

**Joel 3:14 NIV-** Multitudes, multitudes in the valley of decision! For the day of the LORD is near in the valley of decision.

> **HEM-** The so-called Negro has been made so blind, deaf and dumb by them that even the intellectual blacks now are blind and seek to make love and friendship with the people of the devil and satan. The day of decision between the dark races or nations was begun by God Himself in the Person of Master Fard Muhammad, to Whom be praised forever, as is prophesied in the Bible: "Multitudes in the valley of decision, for the day [before or by 1970] of the Lord is near in the valley of decision" (Joel 3:14).[177]

---

[176] Muhammad, *Message to the Blackman in America*, 268.
[177] Ibid., 267-268

# Chapter XVIII:

## Obadiah

**Obadiah 1:15 KJV-** For the day of the LORD is near upon all the heathen: as thou hast done, it shall be done unto thee: thy reward shall return upon thine own head.

**Obadiah 1:15 NIV-** The day of the LORD is near for all nations. As you have done, it will be done to you; your deeds will return upon your own head.

> **HEM-** Bible, Obad. 15, "...As thou has done, it shall be done unto thee." America has done the worst work of deceiving other peoples and making false friendships with them. Now her turn has come. No one wants to trust her for friendship, for she has deceived many nations.[178]

---

[178] Muhammad, *The Fall of America*, 108.

# Chapter XIV:

## Jonah

**Jonah 2:2-4 KJV-** And said, I cried by reason of mine affliction unto the LORD, and he heard me; out of the belly of hell cried I, and thou heardest my voice. For thou hadst cast me into the deep, in the midst of the seas; and the floods compassed me about: all thy billows and thy waves passed over me. Then I said, I am cast out of thy sight; yet I will look again toward thy holy temple.

**Jonah 2:2-4 NIV-** He said: "In my distress I called to the LORD, and he answered me. From the depths of the grave I called for help, and you listened to my cry. You hurled me into the deep, into the very heart of the seas, and the currents swirled about me; all your waves and breakers swept over me. I said, "I have been banished from your sight; yet I will look again toward your holy temple."

> **HEM-** It was by prayer and the turning in the right direction (toward the Holy Temple Mecca) that delivered Jonah from the belly of the fish (Jonah 2:2-4) which is only a type of us here in America (the antitypical fish) who has swallowed us. Our prayers will be speedily heard and Allah will fight our battles against our enemies and bring them to disgrace.[179]

---

[179] Muhammad, *Message to the Blackman*, 141

# Chapter XX:

## Nahum

The book contains the "vision of Nahum" (1:1), whose name means "comfort" and is related to the name Nehemiah, meaning "The Lord comforts" or "comfort of the Lord." (Nineveh's fall, which is Nahum's theme, would bring comfort to Judah.) Nothing is known about him except his hometown (Elkosh), and even its general location is uncertain. [180]

**Nahum 3:5 KJV-** Woe to the bloody city! it is all full of lies and robbery; the prey departeth not; The noise of a whip, and the noise of the rattling of the wheels, and of the prancing horses, and of the jumping chariots.

**Nahum 3:5 NIV-** Woe to the city of blood, full of lies, full of plunder, never without victims! The crack of whips, the clatter of wheels, galloping horses and jolting chariots!

> **HEM-** "Woe to the bloody city! It is all full of lies and robbery; the prey departeth not; The noise of a whip, and the noise of the rattling of the wheels, and of the prancing horses, and of the jumping chariots." (Nahum 3:1,2) America answers this prophecy of the ruins of ancient Ninevah. Ninevah was full of lies and robbery; so is America. "The prey departeth not." The poor so-called Negroes in America are the prey and they refuse to depart from America regardless of the evil treatment they receive. Though the whips and the clubs of their enemy are heard night and day upon the heads and

---

[180] Kenneth L. Baker and G. Herbert Livingston, *Introduction: Nahum*, in *New International Version Study Bible* (Grand Rapids, MI: Zondervan, 2002), 1403.

backs of the prey (so-called Negroes), they still do not desire to depart from America.[181]

**Nahum 3:5 KJV-** Behold, I am against thee, saith the LORD of hosts; and I will discover thy skirts upon thy face, and I will shew the nations thy nakedness, and the kingdoms thy shame.

**Nahum 3:5 NIV-** I am against you," declares the LORD Almighty. "I will lift your skirts over your face. I will show the nations your nakedness and the kingdoms your shame."

> **HEM-** As the Bible teaches us "God will pull the covering off of the covered and show the nations his (white race's) shame" (Nah. 3:5). If the white man had not been uncovered by Almighty God Allah Who Came in the Person of Master Fard Muhammad, to Whom Praises are Due forever, I do not see any cover left for the white man's skin! By Allah (God) Pulling the cover off of the white race this makes it possible for us, the Black People who were Deaf to the knowledge of the truth, to See the natural characteristics of this deadly white enemy of the Black Man.[182]

---

[181] Muhammad, *The Fall of America*, 116.
[182] Ibid., 40-41.

# Chapter XXI:

## Habakkuk

The whole of the third chapter of Habakkuk is devoted to the coming and work of God against our enemies and our deliverance. We must not take our enemies for our spiritual guides lest we regret it. You are already deceived by them. Why seek to follow them and their evil doings; if I would say that God is not a man, I would be a liar before Him and stand to be condemned. Remember! You look forward to seeing God or the coming of the "Son of Man" (a man from a man) and not the coming of a "spirit." Let that one among you who believes God is other than man prove it! [183]

**Habakkuk 2:12 KJV-** Woe to him that buildeth a town with blood, and stablisheth a city by iniquity!

**Habakkuk 2:12 NIV-** Woe to him who builds a city with bloodshed and establishes a town by crime!

> **HEM-** She is full of blood from murdered people. She also fills another prophecy made in Habakkuk 2:12: "Woe to him that buildeth a town with blood, and stablisheth a city by iniquity!" America was founded and built with blood and established by iniquity. She killed the aboriginal inhabitants (Indians) to establish herself as an independent people at the great loss of lives of the original owners. Her great progress has been made by the work of iniquity. She has robbed

---

[183] Muhammad, *Message to the Blackman*, 7.

many people; and the blood of her slaves, the so-called Negroes, has stained the earth here and elsewhere, stained by her hands.[184]

**Habakkuk 3:3 KJV-** God came from Teman, and the Holy One from mount Paran. Selah. His glory covered the heavens, and the earth was full of his praise.

**Habakkuk 3:3 NIV-** God came from Teman, The Holy One from Mount Paran. Selah. His glory covered the heavens, And the earth was full of His praise.

> **HEM-** According to the dictionary of the Bible: Teman, a son of Esau by Adah (Gen. 36:11, 15, 42) and in I Chron. 1:36, now if Habakkuk saw God come or coming from the sons of Esau (Eliphaz), then God must be a man and not a spook. If Habakkuk's (3:3) prophecy refers to some country, town, or city, if there be any truth at all in this prophecy, then we can say that this prophet saw God as a material being, belonging to the human family of the earth-and not to a spirit (ghost). In the same chapter and verse, Habakkuk saw the Holy One from Mount Paran. This is also earthly, somewhere in Arabia. Here the Bible makes a difference between God and another person who is called the Holy One. Which one should we take for our God? For one is called God, while another One is called Holy One. The Holy One: His glory covered the heavens and the earth was full of His praise. It has been a long time since the earth was full of praise for a Holy One. Even to this hour, the people do not care

---

[184] Muhammad, *The Fall of America*, 116.

for Holy People and will persecute and kill the Holy One, if God does not intervene.[185]

**HEM-** The Holy One coming from Mount Paran (Habakkuk 3:3) is not a spirit, but God in person. Jesus referred to Him as being the Son of man (Matt. 24:27)- not the Son of Mary, Whom He was and whom the Christians teach us to look forward to seeing on the last day. If there is or was any truth in looking forward to seeing the return of Jesus (Mary's Son) whom the Bible claims was killed two thousand years ago, what contradicts this prophecy of the coming of the Son of Man? The prophecy of the coming of the Son of Man by Jesus compares with other prophets, and especially Habakkuk 3:3. 'Jesus saw the coming of the Son of Man as a light coming from the East that shineth unto the West.' 'Habakkuk also saw the Holy One as being a light as well as being Holy' (Habakkuk 3:4).

Some of the Arab scholars say that the Holy One mentioned by Habakkuk (3:3) coming from Mount Paran refers to Muhammad- and they are right. But it does not refer to the Muhammad of the past but to the One Muhammad prophesied of in the Sunnah who came from His family in His name under the title, 'Mahdi' (meaning the Guide, the Restorer of the Kingdom of Righteousness).[186]

**Habakkuk 3:4 KJV-** And his brightness was as the light; he had horns coming out of his hand: and there was the hiding of his power.

---

[185] Muhammad, *Message to the Blackman,* 7. Also see, Muhammad, *Our Saviour Has Arrived,* 68. See footnote 27.
[186] Muhammad, *Our Saviour Has Arrived,* 70-71.

**Habakkuk 3:4 NIV-** His brightness was like the light; He had rays flashing from His hand, And there His power was hidden.

> **HEM-** In the fourth verse of the above chapter, it says, "He had horns coming out of his hands; and there was the hiding of His power." Such science to represent the God's power could confuse the ignorant masses of the world. Two gods are here represented at the same time. (It is good that God makes Himself manifest to the ignorant world today.)[187]

**Habakkuk 3:13 KJV-** Thou wentest forth for the salvation of thy people, even for salvation with thine anointed; thou woundedst the head out of the house of the wicked, by discovering the foundation unto the neck. Selah.

**Habakkuk 3:13 NIV-** You came out to deliver your people, to save your anointed one. You crushed the leader of the land of wickedness, you stripped him from head to foot. Selah.

> **HEM-** The 13th verse should clear the way for such undertaking; for it tells us why all these great things took place on the coming of the Holy One from Mount Paran. It says: "Thou wentest forth for the salvation of thy people (not for all people) for the salvation with thine anointed (His Apostle). He wounded the head out of the house of the wicked by discovering the foundation unto the neck (by exposing the truth and ruling powers of the wicked race of devils)." "Cushan" represents the Black Nation which is afflicted by the white race. "The curtains of the land of Midian" could

---

[187] Muhammad, *Message to the Blackman*, 7.

mean the falsehood spread over the people by the white race and their leaders trembling from being exposed by the truth. "The mountains" represent the great, rich and powerful political men of the wicked; they also are trembling and being divided and scattered over the earth. "The Holy One" is God in person and not a spirit![188]

**HEM-** I and my followers have been suffering cruel persecution-police brutality- for the past 34 years; but have patience, my dear followers, for release is in sight. Even those who made mockery of you shall be paid fully for his or her mockery; for the prophesy of Habakkuk is true if understood; wherein he says: 'Thou wentest forth for the salvation of Thy people' [the so-called Negroes] (3:13)[189]

---

[188] Muhammad, *Message to the Blackman*, 7.
[189] Ibid., 6.

# Chapter XXII:

## Zechariah

**Zechariah 14:9 KJV-** And the LORD shall be king over all the earth: in that day shall there be one LORD, and his name one.

**Zechariah 14:9 NIV-** The LORD will be king over the whole earth. On that day there will be one LORD, and his name the only name.

> **HEM-** Our God is One today, as we had only one God in the beginning. 'In that day (this is the day) shall there be One Lord and His name One' (Zecharaiah 14:9). This refers to the time when the true God is made manifest. Before His manifestation, the people worship what they think or what they want to be their god. The devil's teaching is a division of gods- three gods into one god. The Hindus have many gods.[190]

---

[190] Muhammad, *Our Saviour Has Arrived,* 67.

# Chapter XXIII:

## Malachi

The book is ascribed to Malachi, whose name means "my messenger." Since the term occurs in 3:1, and since both prophets and priests were called messengers of the Lord (see 2:7; Hag 1:13), some have thought "Malachi" to be only a title that tradition has given the author. The view has been supported by appeal to the pre-Christian Greek translation of the OT (the Septuagint), which translates the term in 1:1 "his messenger" rather than as a proper noun. The matter, however, remains uncertain, and it is still very likely that Malachi was in fact the author's name.[191]

**Malachi 3:3 KJV-** And he shall sit as a refiner and purifier of silver: and he shall purify the sons of Levi, and purge them as gold and silver, that they may offer unto the LORD an offering in righteousness.

**Malachi 3:3 NIV-** He will sit as a refiner and purifier of silver; he will purify the Levites and refine them like gold and silver. Then the LORD will have men who will bring offerings in righteousness.

> **HEM-** God referred to this internal and external cleansing in these words, (Mal. 3:3) 'He shall sit as a refiner and purifier of silver. He shall purge the priesthood of the people that they may offer unto the Lord an offering in righteousness.' Islam comes to

---

[191] John H. Stek and Herbert Wolfe, *Introduction: Malachi*, in *New International Version Study Bible* (Grand Rapids, MI: Zondervan, 2002), 1448.

reform the so-called Negro and to save him from God's destruction of the enemy devil. Islam, if carried into practice by you and me, will eradicate all such things as slums because it is people who create slums. When we ask other people to clean up our own filthy houses, we are disgracing our own intelligence and decency. But the sense of dignity that Islam puts into us forces us to qualify ourselves in intelligence and dignity and to remain qualified. This is the qualification we need.[192]

---

[192] Muhammad, *Our Saviour Has Arrived*, 142-143.

# Chapter XXIV:

## New Testament

## Matthew

**Matthew 1:21 KJV-** And she shall bring forth a son, and thou shalt call his name JESUS: for he shall save his people from their sins.

**Matthew 1:21 NIV-** She will give birth to a son, and you are to give him the name Jesus, because he will save his people from their sins.

> **HEM-** The Great Mahdi, the Saviour of His People Bible Mt. 1:21 prophesied that He Was Born to Save His People from sin. They were guilty of the same sin as that of their evil teacher, for they practiced the same sin. Upon the coming of God, the Son of Man, He being the Just Judge of Man and man-kind, He forgave us our sins because we are not guilty of that which we did not know. The mankind (white man) taught us from the cradle to follow after them. They separated us from our Original People of Asia and Africa in order to do a thorough job of making us other than ourselves, the Original Black Man.[193]

**Matthew 2:8 KJV-** And he sent them to Bethlehem, and said, Go and search diligently for the young child; and when ye have found him, bring me word again, that I may come and worship him also.

---

[193] Muhammad, *Our Saviour Has Arrived*, 184-185.

**Matthew 2:8 NIV-** He sent them to Bethlehem and said, "Go and make a careful search for the child. As soon as you find him, report to me, so that I too may go and worship him".

> **HEM-** The Bible, Matt. 2:8, teaches that on his birth, when Herod heard of it, sent spies to ascertain the truth of the news that Mary had given birth to a child called Jesus. He told them to bring word to him that he may go and worship him. But by no means did he intend to give a true worship and recognition of Mary's son, Jesus. He desired death for the son because he had read the Torah and in it is a prophecy of the Coming and Birth of a Ruler who would be King of the Jews. He felt that his authorities and rule would be threatened and brought to a naught if this was the baby prophesied of.[194]

**Matthew 2:13 KJV-** And when they were departed, behold, the angel of the Lord appeareth to Joseph in a dream, saying, Arise, and take the young child and his mother, and flee into Egypt, and be thou there until I bring the word: for Herod will seek the young child to destroy him.

**Matthew 2:13 NIV-** And when they were departed, behold, the angel of the Lord appeareth to Joseph in a dream, saying, Arise, and take the young child and his mother, and flee into Egypt, and be thou there until I bring the word: for Herod will seek the young child to destroy him.

---

[194] Muhammad, *Our Saviour Has Arrived*, 161.

The fleeing of Mary with her son to Egypt and Joseph's aiding her to make haste to Egypt Bible Matt. 2:13, is a beautiful sign of the so-called American Negro fleeing out of America to the open arms of the Muslim world. The King, Herod, desired most of all to kill Jesus in his infancy. Bible, Rev. 12:4 tells us that the dragon stood before the woman. The woman here represents the Messenger of God. The child represents the followers of the Messenger. [195]

**Matthew 4:4 KJV-** But he answered and said, It is written, Man shall not live by bread alone, but by every word that proceedeth out of the mouth of God.

**Matthew 4:4 NIV-** Jesus answered, "It is written: 'Man does not live on bread alone, but on every word that comes from the mouth of God.

> **HEM-** Another {prayer} is: "Give us this day our daily bread." Here again, the words "this day" could lead one to believe that on that day the prayer was given, there was a shortage of bread, or that the Christians' prayers seek their physical bread first and spiritual bread last, even though the Bible says "You first seek the Kingdom of Heaven and all these things shall be added unto you" (Luke 12:31). In another place it says "Man shall not live by bread alone, but by every word that proceedeth out of the mouth of God" (Matthew 4:4) These scriptures are contrary to the prayer, although it stands true of the Christians who seek

---

[195] Muhammad, *Our Saviour Has Arrived*, 162.

bread, swine's flesh (the poison), whiskey, wine and beer first, and pray for spiritual food last.[196]

**Matthew 4:9 KJV-** And saith unto him, "All these things will I give thee, if thou wilt fall down and worship me."

**Matthew 4:9 NIV-** "All this I will give you," he said, "if you will bow down and worship me."

> **HEM-** We are justified in taking it if the white man gave us a billion or a hundred billion dollars. We deserve it. But we are not justified to sell our lives for such a gift in this day and time. Declare yourself a Muslim and see how much the devil will give you. He would say, "We will give it to you if you preach that we are not the devil." We would answer, "that is just the same as saying, if you do not teach the truth of me, so that I can continue to deceive the world of your kind, I will help you." "Remember what the Bible teaches us that Satan said to Jesus, "...All these things will I give thee, if thou wilt fall down and worship me." Matt: 4:9. And he showed him the kingdoms of the world.[197]

**Matthew 15:14 KJV-** Let them alone: they be blind leaders of the blind. And if the blind lead the blind, both shall fall into the ditch.

**Matthew 15:14 NIV-** Leave them; they are blind guides. If a blind man leads a blind man, both will fall into a pit.

---

[196] Muhammad, *Message to the Blackman*, 155.
[197] Muhammad, *The Fall of America*, 64.

> **HEM-** How can such a spiritually blind person believe when he does not understand what he is reading himself? The Jesus was right when he prophesied that the blind cannot lead the blind Mt. 15:14. This is the classification which he gave to the blind preachers and their blind followers.[198]

**Mathew 15:24 KJV-** But he answered and said, I am not sent but unto the lost sheep of the house of Israel.

**Matthew 15:24 NIV-** He answered, "I was sent only to the lost sheep of Israel."

> **HEM-** If Jesus said that He was sent (Matt. 15:24 and John 4:34), then He cannot claim to be equal of His sender. God is not sent by anyone; He is a self-sender.[199]

**Matthew 21:33, 41-42 KJV- 33** Hear another parable: There was a certain householder, which planted a vineyard, and hedged it round about, and digged a winepress in it, and built a tower, and let it out to husbandmen, and went into a far country. **41** He will bring those wretches to a wretched end, "they replied, "and he will rent the vineyard to other tenants, who will give him his share of the crop at harvest time." **42** Jesus saith unto them, Did ye never read in the scriptures, The stone which the builders rejected, the same is become the head of the corner: this is the Lord's doing, and it is marvellous in our eyes?

---

[198] Muhammad, *Our Saviour Has Arrived*, 132.
[199] Muhammad, *Message to the Blackman*, 27.

**Matthew 21:33, 41-42 NIV- 33** Listen to another parable: There was a landowner who planted a vineyard. He put a wall around it, dug a winepress in it and built a watchtower. Then he rented the vineyard to some farmers and went away on a journey. **41** They say unto him, He will miserably destroy those wicked men, and will let out his vineyard unto other husbandmen, which shall render him the fruits in their seasons. **42** Jesus said to them, "Have you never read in the Scriptures:" 'The stone the builders rejected has become the capstone; the Lord has done this, and it is marvelous in our eyes.

> **HEM-** The world of Satan, the devil, did not convert people to God according to the parable of the wicked husbands whom the Lord let His vineyard out to (Matthew 21:33; 41). In the 42nd verse of the same chapter, Jesus makes another parable of the true worshippers under the 'stone that the builders rejected'; that it became the "headstone." It is the so-called Negroes who have been rejected by the builders of governments (civilizations) who are now destined to become the head in the new world (or government) under the Divine Supreme Being in person.
>
> It is natural to say that God is the Spirit of Truth, of Life. It is natural to say such and such a one is a liar, but where there is no one to tell a lie, there is no liar. So it is with truth or the spirit of truth. If there is nothing to produce the spirit, there is no spirit; nor can we know the truth without someone to teach the truth. Where there is man, there is the spirit. Where there is no man, there is no spirit, for the spirit cannot produce itself. We cannot expect to see that which cannot be seen. A spirit cannot be seen, only felt. It is like electricity. Electricity is a power produced by friction

from a substance that has such power (electric) in it produced by the sun and moon upon the earth. It is not seen, but we know what makes it. So it is with God.[200]

## Matthew Chpt. 24:

**HEM-** The Signs of the Coming of God- "And Jesus said unto them see ye not these things? Verily I say unto you, There shall not be left here one stone upon another, that shall not be torn down" [Matt. 24:] This chapter refers to the signs of the judgment of the wicked world. Jesus pointed out examples of the destruction of the Jewish Temple or synagogue, and the historians wrote that the Romans came about 70 years later- after the death of Jesus- and sacked Jerusalem. Really, this was not the end of Jesus' prophecy of the destruction of Jerusalem by the Romans for all the stones were not overthrown by Rome.[201]

**Matthew 24:27 KJV-** For as the lightning cometh out of the east, and shineth even unto the west; so shall also the coming of the Son of man be.

**Matthew 24:27 NIV-** For as lightning that comes from the east is visible even in the west, so will be the coming of the Son of Man.

> **HEM-** On that day, a Son of a Man will sit to judge men according to their works. Who is the Father of this Son, coming to a judge the world? Is His Father of

---

[200] Muhammad, *Our Saviour Has Arrived*, 65-66.
[201] Muhammad, *Message to the Blackman*, 286.

flesh and blood or is He a "spirit"? Where is this Son coming from? Prophet Jesus said: "He will come from the East." (Matt. 24:27) from the land and people of Islam, where all of the former prophets came from. Jesus compared His coming as "the lightning." Of course, lightning cannot be seen or heard at a great distance. The actual light (the Truth) which "shineth even unto the West," is our day sun. But the Son of Man's coming is like both the lightning and our day sun.

His work of the resurrection of the mentally dead so-called Negroes, and judgment between truth and falsehood, is compared with lightning- on an instant. His swiftness in condemning the falsehood is like the sudden flash of lightning in a dark place, where the darkness has blinded the people so that they cannot find the "right way" out. The sudden "flash of lightning" enables them to see that they are off from the "right path." They walk a few steps toward the "right way" but soon have to stop and wait for another bright flash. What they actually need is the light of the Sun (God in Person), that they may clearly see their way. The lightning does more than flash a light. It is also destructive, striking whom Allah pleases, or taking property as well as lives. The brightness of its flashes almost blinds the eyes. [202]

**HEM-** My greatest and only desire is to bring true understanding of the word of God, His prophets and the scriptures, which the prophets were sent with, pertaining to the lost- found people (the American so-called Negroes) of God and the judgment of the world. You must forget about ever seeing the return of Jesus, Who was here 2,000 years ago. Set your heart on

---

[202] Muhammad, *Message to the Blackman*, 12.

seeing the One that He prophesied would come at the end of the present world's time (the white race's time).[203]

**HEM-** The Holy One coming from Mount Paran (Habakkuk 3:3) is not a spirit, but God in person. Jesus referred to Him as being the Son of man (Matt. 24:27) not the Son of Mary, Whom He was and whom the Christians teach us to look forward to seeing on the last day. If there is or was any truth in looking forward to seeing the return of Jesus (Mary's Son) whom the Bible claims was killed two thousand years ago, what contradicts this prophecy of the coming of the Son of Man?[204]

**Matthew 24:28 KJV-** For wheresoever the carcass is, there will the eagles be gathered together.

**Matthew 24:28 NIV-** Wherever there is a carcass, there the vultures will gather.

**HEM-** Woe, woe to America! Her day is near, and she shall be visited. Your enemies warn you that the third and final World War will be decided in your own country and not in theirs. Remember the old Bible's sayings: "Wheresoever the carcass is, there will be eagles gathered together" (Matt. 24:28). You must understand and know to whom the parable is directed.[205]

---

[203] Muhammad, *Message to the Blackman*, 10
[204] Muhammad, *Our Saviour Has Arrived*, 70.
[205] Muhammad, *Message to the Blackman*, 300. In *Message to the Blackman in America*, 25:28 is improperly cited. The correct scripture is 24:28.

**Matthew 24:30 KJV-** And then shall appear the sign of the Son of man in heaven: and then shall all the tribes of the earth mourn, and they shall see the Son of man coming in the clouds of heaven with power and great glory.

**Matthew 24:30 NIV-** At that time the sign of the Son of Man will appear in the sky, and all the nations of the earth will mourn. They will see the Son of Man coming on the clouds of the sky, with power and great glory.

> **HEM-** Here in the plainest words is the Son of Man on the Judgment Day. We are not told by either Moses or Jesus to look for God on Judgment Day to be anything other than man. Spirits and spooks cannot be the judge of man's affairs. Man is material, of the earth. How long will you be ignorant of the reality of God? You are poisoned by the devil's touch. Why are you looking for a God that is not flesh and blood as you are? Spirits can only be found in another being like yourself. What pleasure would you have in an invisible world? And on the other hand what pleasure would spirits have in this material universe of ours? Your very nature is against your being anything other than a human being.[206]

> **HEM-** I think I have made it clear to you that if we look forward to seeing or meeting God, He must be in the form of a man. The Christians' Bible bears me witness that God is a man of flesh and blood. The Bible predicts God coming as a man (Luke 21:27; Matthew 24:30; Revelation 1:7, 14:15). There is much

---

[206] Muhammad, *Message to the Blackman*, 19.

proof in the Bible to support my claim that God is man. That is, if you want proof.[207]

**Matthew 24:36 KJV-** But of that day and hour knoweth no man, no, not the angels of heaven, but my Father only.

**Matthew 24:36 NIV-** No one knows about that day or hour, not even the angels in heaven, nor the Son, but only the Father.

> **HEM-** He is called the *"Son of Man,"* the *"Christ,"* the *"Comforter."* You are really foolish to be looking to see the return of the Prophet Jesus. It is the same as looking for the return of Abraham, Moses and Muhammad. All of these prophets prophesied the coming of Allah or one with equal power, under many names. You must remember that Jesus could not have been referring to Himself as returning to the people in the last days. He prophesied or another's coming who was much greater than He. Jesus even acknowledged that He did not know when the hour would come in these words; "But of that day and hour knoweth no man, no, not the angels of heaven, but my Father only." (Matt. 24:36) If He were the one to return at the end of the world, surely He would have had knowledge of the time of His return, the knowledge of the hour. But He left Himself out of that knowledge and placed it where it belonged, as all the others prophets had done. No has been able to tell us the hour of the judgment. No one but He, the great all wise God, Allah. He is called the "Son of Man," the "Mahdi", the "Christ". The prophets, Jesus included, could only foretell those things which would serve as signs, signs that would

---

[207] Muhammad, *Our Saviour Has Arrived*, 72.

precede such a great one's coming to judge the world. The knowledge of the hour of judgment is with the Executor only.[208]

**Matthew 24:37-39 KJV-** But as the days of Noah were, so shall also the coming of the Son of man be. For as in the days that were before the flood they were eating and drinking, marrying and giving in marriage, until the day that Noe entered into the ark, And knew not until the flood came, and took them all away; so shall also the coming of the Son of man be.

**Matthew 24:37-39 NIV-** As it was in the days of Noah, so it will be at the coming of the Son of Man. For in the days before the flood, people were eating and drinking, marrying and giving in marriage, up to the day Noah entered the ark; and they knew nothing about what would happen until the flood came and took them all away. That is how it will be at the coming of the Son of Man.

> **HEM-** The prophets teach us to let the past judgments of people, their cities, and their warners serve as a lesson, or sign, of the last judgment and its warners. Noah did not know the hour of the flood. Lot did not know the Hour of Sodom and Gomorrah until the Executors had arrived, and Jesus prophesied (Matt. 24:37- 39): "It will be the same in the last judgment of the world of Satan." You have gone astray because of your misunderstanding of the scripture, the Prophet Jesus, and the coming of God to judge the world. My corrections are not accepted.[209]

---

[208] Muhammad, *Message to the Blackman*, 10-11
[209] Ibid., 11.

**HEM-** In the day of Noah, the children of the Sodomites came out happy that morning, and that was the end. They saw a cloud making up. They just considered that it was a regular rain cloud, but that was the end! In the Bible prophecy of Jesus (Matt. 24:38,39), "For as in the days that were before the flood they were eating and drinking, marrying and giving in marriage, until the day that Noah entered into the ark, and knew not until the flood came, and took them all away." In the time of Noah, the people of Noah were having parties as you are doing today, and that day was the end.[210]

**Matthew 25:32 KJV-** And before him shall be gathered all nations: and he shall separate them one from another, as a shepherd divideth his sheep from the goats.

**Matthew 25:32 NIV-** All the nations will be gathered before him, and he will separate the people one from another as a shepherd separates the sheep from the goats.

**HEM-** The Bible says (Mt. 25:32) 'Before Him shall be gathered all nations.' The Holy Qur'an says, 'you shall see all nations kneeling before Him and they shall be judged out of their own books.' The government keeps a record of their governmental accounts. They have books in the library and in the courts which tell how they have ruled the people. They have a record of how they have judged the people.[211]

---

[210] Muhammad, *The Fall of America*, 250.
[211] Muhammad, *Our Saviour Has Arrived*, 186. See also Isaiah 45:23 and Deuteronomy 18:15.

**Matthew 27:46 KJV-** And about the ninth hour Jesus cried with a loud voice, saying, Eli, Eli, lama sabachthani? that is to say, My God, my God, why hast thou forsaken me?

**Matthew 27:46 NIV-** About the ninth hour Jesus cried out in a loud voice, "Eloi, Eloi, lama sabachthani?" which means, "My God, my God, why have you forsaken me?"

> **HEM-** It is foolish to believe in three gods- foolish to make Jesus the Son and the equal of His Father (the one of 2,000 years ago). If Jesus said in His suffering "My God, My God, why hast Thou forsaken Me?" (Matt. 27:46) then most surely He did not recognize Himself as being the equal of God, and no other scripture shows Jesus as the equal of God. [212]

---

[212] Muhammad, *Message to the Blackman*, 27.

# Chapter XXV:

## Mark

**Mark 5:2-13 KJV-** And when he was come out of the ship, immediately there met him out of the tombs a man with an unclean spirit, Who had his dwelling among the tombs; and no man could bind him, no, not with chains: Because that he had been often bound with fetters and chains, and the chains had been plucked asunder by him, and the fetters broken in pieces: neither could any man tame him. And always, night and day, he was in the mountains, and in the tombs, crying, and cutting himself with stones. But when he saw Jesus afar off, he ran and worshipped him, And cried with a loud voice, and said, What have I to do with thee, Jesus, thou Son of the most high God? I adjure thee by God, that thou torment me not. For he said unto him, Come out of the man, thou unclean spirit. And he asked him, What is thy name? And he answered, saying, My name is Legion: for we are many. And he besought him much that he would not send them away out of the country. Now there was there nigh unto the mountains a great herd of swine feeding. And all the devils besought him, saying, Send us into the swine, that we may enter into them. And forthwith Jesus gave them leave. And the unclean spirits went out, and entered into the swine: and the herd ran violently down a steep place into the sea, (they were about two thousand;) and were choked in the sea.

**Mark 5:2-13 NIV-** When Jesus got out of the boat, a man with an evil spirit came from the tombs to meet him. This man lived in the tombs, and no one could bind him any more, not even with a chain. For he had often been chained hand and foot, but he tore the chains apart and broke the irons on his feet. No one was strong enough to subdue him. Night and day among the tombs and in the hills he would cry out and cut himself with stones. When he saw Jesus from a distance, he ran and fell on his knees in front of him. He shouted at the top of his voice, "What do you want with me, Jesus, Son of the Most High God? Swear to God that you won't torture me!" For Jesus had said to him, "Come out of this man, you evil spirit!" Then Jesus asked him, "What is your name?" "My name is Legion," he replied, "for we are many." And he begged Jesus again and again not to send them out of the area. A large herd of pigs was feeding on the nearby hillside. The demons begged Jesus, "Send us among the pigs; allow us to go into them." He gave them permission, and the evil spirits came out and went into the pigs. The herd, about two thousand in number, rushed down the steep bank into the lake and were drowned.

**HEM-** Read the story in the Bible in which Jesus met a man who was possessed of evil spirits. When the evil spirits recognized Jesus to be from God- knowing they would have no chance to contend with him over their presence in the man where they did not belong- they pleaded with Jesus to let them go into the swine, and Jesus agreed. The man who was possessed of evil spirits was none other than the American so-called Negro. The evil spirits in him are from the white race, who made him eat the divinely-prohibited flesh of the swine. The devils were allowed to go into the swine.

They ran down a steep place into a lake or sea and perished.[213]

**HEM-** The white race is mentioned in a teaching of the Bible in St. Mark, Chapter 5:13, in the evil spirits taken out of the man, mentioned there of being possessed with evil spirits and the spirits begging Jesus to allow them to go into the hog. Here, the two are associated with each other- the evil spirits and the hog. The hog was not made evil by nature, but by nature, it was made to serve the evil person. Therefore, both were made for each other.[214]

**HEM-** In the Bible and the Holy Qur'an, it is the Divine will of God that the pig should not be eaten and God has never changed this instruction, despite the white man's setting up governmental bureaus to grade and approve the selling of pork.[215]

**HEM-** You can read a parable concerning this filthy swine: Jesus found a man possessed of evil spirits, and wanting to relieve the man of such evil spirits, he sent the evil spirits (devils) out of the man into the swine. The preachers (representatives of the son of God) and the priests know this to be true, but they preach that it is all right now to eat swine- and still say they are the beloved of Jesus. How could they be when they broke the laws of God by eating the swine? Nowhere in the scriptures does it bid us to break the law that God set up for this prohibited flesh.[216]

---

[213] Muhammad, *How to Eat to Live I*, 72-73.
[214] Muhammad, *How to Eat to Live I*, 132.
[215] Ibid., 114. See also Leviticus 11:7-8 and Deuteronomy 14:8.
[216] Muhammad, *How to Eat to Live I*, 69.

**Mark 12:32 KJV-** And the scribe said unto him, Well, Master, thou hast said the truth: for there is one God; and there is none other but he.

**Mark 12:32 NIV-** "Well said, teacher," the man replied. "You are right in saying that God is one and there is no other but him".

> **HEM-** If Jesus said that he was sent (Matt. 15:24 and John 4:34) then he cannot claim to be equal of His sender. God is not sent by anyone; He is a self-sender. He says in Isaiah (44:81-45:22): "Is there a God besides Me? I know not any.(45:22)" In another place He states "I am God, there is none else.(46:9)" Also, "One God and none other." (Mark 12:32)[217]

**Mark 13:20 KJV-** And except that the Lord had shortened those days, no flesh should be saved: but for the elect's sake, whom he hath chosen, he hath shortened the days.

**Mark 13:20 NIV-** If the Lord had not cut short those days, no one would survive. But for the sake of the elect, whom he has chosen, he has shortened them.

> **HEM-** At such time as the destruction of America, if Allah (God) has chosen some of the people of America (the Black slave) to be His people, there would not have been any flesh saved from America. The Bible, Mk. 13:20, teaches us, "And except that the Lord had shortened those days, no flesh should be saved; but for

---

[217] Muhammad, *Message to the Blackman in America*, 27.

the elect's sake, whom he hath chosen, he hath shortened the days." [218]

---

[218] Muhammad, *The Fall of America*, 223.

# Chapter XXVI:

## Luke

**Luke 6:27-29 KJV-** But I say unto you which hear, Love your enemies, do good to them which hate you, Bless them that curse you, and pray for them which despitefully use you. And unto him that smiteth thee on the one cheek offer also the other; and him that taketh away thy cloak forbid not to take thy coat also.

**Luke 6:27-29 NIV-** "But I tell you who hear me: Love your enemies, do good to those who hate you, bless those who curse you, pray for those who mistreat you. If someone strikes you on one cheek, turn to him the other also. If someone takes your cloak, do not stop him from taking your tunic.

> **HEM-** Regardless of our sins that we have committed in following and obeying our slave-masters, Allah (God) forgives it all today, if we, the so-called Negroes, will turn to Him and our own kind. If the wicked can rejoice over the finding of his lost and strayed animal, or a piece of silver, or a son who had a desire to leave home and practice the evil habits of strangers, how much more should Allah and the nation of Islam rejoice over finding us, their people, who have been lost from them for 400 years following other than our own kind? We, being robbed so thoroughly of the knowledge of self and kind, are opposed to our own salvation in favor of our enemies, and I here quote another poison addition of the slavery teachings of the Bible: Love your enemies, bless them who curse you,

pray for those who spitefully use you, him that smiteth thee on one cheek offer the other cheek, him that taketh (rob) away thy cloak, forbid not to take away thy coat also. (Luke 6:27-28-29). The slave-masters couldn't have found a better teaching for their protection against the slaves possible dissatisfaction of their master's brutal treatment. It is against the very nature of God and man, and other life, to love their enemies. Would God ask us to do that which He, Himself, can't do? He hates his enemies so much that He tells us that He is going to destroy them in hell fire, along with those of us who follow His enemies.[219]

**Luke 12:31 KJV-** But rather seek ye the kingdom of God; and all these things shall be added unto you.

**Luke 12:31 NIV-** But seek his kingdom, and these things will be given to you as well.

> **HEM-** Another {prayer} is: "Give us this day our daily bread." Here again, the words "this day" could lead one to believe that on that day the prayer was given, there was a shortage of bread, or that the Christians' prayers seek their physical bread first and spiritual bread last, even though the Bible says "You first seek the Kingdom of Heaven and all these things shall be added unto you" (Luke 12:31). In another place it says "Man shall not live by bread alone, but by every word that proceedeth out of the mouth of God" (Matthew 4:4) These scriptures are contrary to the prayer, although it stands true of the Christians who seek

---

[219] Muhammad, *Message to the Blackman*, 96.

bread, swine's flesh (the poison),whiskey, wine and beer first, and pray for spiritual food last.[220]

**Luke 15:1, 11, 21-22 KJV- 1** Then drew near unto him all the publicans and sinners for to hear him. **11** And he said, A certain man had two sons; **21** And the son said unto him, Father, I have sinned against heaven, and in thy sight, and am no more worthy to be called thy son. **22** But the father said to his servants, Bring forth the best robe, and put it on him; and put a ring on his hand, and shoes on his feet.

**Luke 15:1, 11, 21-22 NIV- 1** Now the tax collectors and "sinners" were all gathering around to hear him. **11** Jesus continued: "There was a man who had two sons. **21** "The son said to him, 'Father, I have sinned against heaven and against you. I am no longer worthy to be called your son. **22** "But the father said to his servants, 'Quick! Bring the best robe and put it on him. Put a ring on his finger and sandals on his feet.

> **HEM-** Study the parable of Jesus and the lost sheep, the prodigal son (Luke 15:11, 21, 22), the stone that the builders rejected, the garden taken from the wicked husband and given to another and the mustard seed becoming a tree under which the beast found shade and in which the birds found rest. Know that you, the so-called American Negroes, are divinely promised the Kingdom of Heaven (as it is called) after the destruction of this world. And he said, A certain man had two sons: And the son said unto him, Father, I have sinned against heaven, and in thy sight, and am

---

[220] Muhammad, *Message to the Blackman*, 154-155.

no more worthy to be called thy son. But the father said to his servants, Bring forth the best robe, and put it on him; and put a ring on his hand, and shoes on his feet.[221]

**HEM-** We, the so-called American Negroes, are mentioned in the New Testament under several names and parables. I will name two, the parable of the Lost Sheep and the Prodigal Son (Luke 15:1,11); we could not be described better. Before the coming of Allah (God), we, being blind, deaf and dumb, had mistaken the true meanings of these parables as referring to the Jews. Now, thanks to Almighty God Allah, Who came in the person of Master Fard Muhammad (who be praised forever), who has opened my blinded eyes, and unstopped my ears, loosen the knot in my tongue, and has made us to understand these Bible parables are referring to us, the so-called Negroes and our slave-masters.[222]

**HEM-** We have made the grave mistake of Lazarus and the Prodigal Son, (St. Luke: Chapter 15), the one who was so charmed over the wealth and food of the rich man that he could not leave his gate to seek the same for himself, regardless of the disgraceful condition in which the rich man puts him, even to sending his dogs to attack him. The angels had to come and take him away. The other (Prodigal Son),

---

[221] Muhammad, *Message to the Blackman,* 297. Luke 15:1, 11 are sited here, but there are several periscopes written in Luke 15:1-32, The Parable of the Lost Sheep; The Parable of the Lost Coin; The Parable of the Tenants; The Parable of the Mustard Seed and the Yeast and The Parable of the Lost Son. To understand in context what the Hon. Elijah Muhammad is referring to of the Lost Sheep and of the Prodigal Son, read the entire chapter Luke15:1-32. Some versions of the Bible only contain 31 verses as the NIV. For the "stone the builders rejected", see Psalms 118:72; Matt. 21:42; Mark 12:10; Luke. 20:17; Acts 4:11; 1Peter 2:17 in NIV. See Matt. 21:42; Mark 12:10; Luke. 20:17 in KJV. For references to the mustard seed also see, Matt. 13:31, 17:20. See Mark 4:31, Luke 13:19, Luke 17:6.
[222] Ibid., 95-96. See 139

being tempted by the loose life of strange women, drinking, gambling, and adultery, caused him to love the stranger's way of life so much that it cost him all that he originally possessed (self-independence and Divine Guidance). His Father (God in Person) had to come and be his representative to again meet his brothers, family, and friends. Nothing fits the description of us better, the so-called Negroes (Asiatics).[223]

**HEM-** Abraham's prophecy. But, I ask you to remember: in the parable in the Bible of the rich man and Lazarus- which means none other than the white and Black people of America- the rich man died deprived of authority and wealth. In the anguish of the torment of his loss of wealth and power, the parable refers to the rich man as being in hell. And in this condition, the beggar (Lazarus) saw no hope in begging that once rich man any longer for some of his sumptuous food. Then he turned to go for self (Abraham's). The prophecy which Abraham was the recipient of only means that after 400 years of our enslavement, all these things are coming to pass. I ask you to be in time and accept the truth and do not mix up the truth with falsehood while you know it for the sake of untrue friendship.[224]

**HEM-** The answer (Luke 15:4,6) to the charges made by the proud and unholy Pharisees against Him (God in Person) for eating with His lost-found people whom the Pharisees and their people had made sinners, can't be better. It defends Him and His people (lost and

---

[223] Muhammad, *Message to the Blackman*, 25-26. See 139.
[224] Muhammad, *Our Saviour Has Arrived*, 3-4. See Luke 16:19-32, The Rich Man and Lazarus.

found sheep). He proved their wicked hatred for His love for His people who were lost and He (God) has found them. They (the Pharisees and their people) had more love for a lost and found animal of theirs than they did for the lost and found people of Allah (God).[225]

**Luke 15:6 KJV-** And when he cometh home, he calleth together his friends and neighbours, saying unto them, Rejoice with me; for I have found my sheep which was lost.

**Luke 15:6 NIV-** ... And goes home. Then he calls his friends and neighbors together and says, 'Rejoice with me; I have found my lost sheep.'

> **HEM-** We have parables in the Bible which the writers of the history of Jesus tell us were spoken by Jesus--the Parable of the Lost Sheep and the Prodigal Son -- they returned and became the owners. This only means you and me. Why do not we take our place? Why should we give our babies to the enemy to be destroyed because he says you have nothing to feed them with? Follow me and I will show you: you will get more houses than you need and more money than you can spend. Help me, brothers, and Allah (God) will not deprive you of your good reward. I know you understand. What we do for Allah (God) He will do it for us. In this day and time we are all tried-- the wicked and the righteous are both tried.[226]

---

[225] Muhammad, *Message to the Blackman*, 96. See 139.
[226] Muhammad, *The Fall of America*, 31.

**Luke 16:19-25 KJV-** There was a certain rich man, which was clothed in purple and fine linen, and fared sumptuously every day: And there was a certain beggar named Lazarus, which was laid at his gate, full of sores, And desiring to be fed with the crumbs which fell from the rich man's table: moreover the dogs came and licked his sores. And it came to pass, that the beggar died, and was carried by the angels into Abraham's bosom: the rich man also died, and was buried; And in hell he lift up his eyes, being in torments, and seeth Abraham afar off, and Lazarus in his bosom. And he cried and said, Father Abraham, have mercy on me, and send Lazarus, that he may dip the tip of his finger in water, and cool my tongue; for I am tormented in this flame. But Abraham said, Son, remember that thou in thy lifetime receivedst thy good things, and likewise Lazarus evil things: but now he is comforted, and thou art tormented.


**Luke 16:19-25 NIV-** There was a rich man who was dressed in purple and fine linen and lived in luxury every day. At his gate was laid a beggar named Lazarus, covered with sores and longing to eat what fell from the rich man's table. Even the dogs came and licked his sores. "The time came when the beggar died and the angels carried him to Abraham's side. The rich man also died and was buried. In hell, where he was in torment, he looked up and saw Abraham far away, with Lazarus by his side. So he called to him, "Father Abraham, have pity on me and send Lazarus to dip the tip of his finger in water and cool my tongue, because I am in agony in this fire." "But Abraham replied, 'Son, remember that in your lifetime you received your good things, while Lazarus received bad things, but now he is comforted here and you are in agony.

> It is so strange now today to see that the Black Man of America desires not to be separated from his enemy, but desires that the enemy and himself live together in love of each other, as brothers, while the enemy knows that it cannot be done. But he can use their ignorant love and belief in him to take him to hell with him. Therefore, Allah (God) has to Strike both parties, the white man (devil) and the Black, blind, deaf and dumb lovers of their enemy, with a severe chastisement, in order to open their blind eyes, as he did in Jesus' parable of the rich man and the poor man, Lazarus (Bible Luke 16:19-25). Lazarus refused to give up begging his master for survival until Allah (God) sent a famine on the rich man. The worse famine that man has ever seen is prophesied to come upon America. [227]

**Luke 17:25, 27-30 KJV- 25** But first must he suffer many things, and be rejected of this generation. **27** They did eat, they drank, they married wives, they were given in marriage, until the day that Noah entered into the ark, and the flood came, and destroyed them all. **28** Likewise also as it was in the days of Lot; they did eat, they drank, they bought, they sold, they planted, they builded; **29** But the same day that Lot went out of Sodom it rained fire and brimstone from heaven, and destroyed them all. **30** Even thus shall it be in the day when the Son of man is revealed.

**Luke 17:25, 27-30 NIV- 25** But first he must suffer many things and be rejected by this generation. **27** People were

---

[227] Muhammad, *Our Saviour Has Arrived*, 199.

eating, drinking, marrying and being given in marriage up to the day Noah entered the ark. Then the flood came and destroyed them all. **28** "It was the same in the days of Lot. People were eating and drinking, buying and selling, planting and building. **29** But the day Lot left Sodom, fire and sulfur rained down from heaven and destroyed them all. **30** "It will be just like this on the day the Son of Man is revealed.

> **HEM-** Let us quote another prophecy of Jesus on the coming of the Son of Man: 'But first must He suffer many things, and be rejected of this generation' (Luke 17:25). The words, 'this generation,' is not to be taken to mean the generation in the days of Jesus and His rejecters, the Jews, two thousand years ago. It means the people and generation of the Son of Man who would reject Him in His day of coming to reclaim His lost-found people; and at the same time, suffer persecution of Self and His teachings as Jesus was by the same enemies in His time. For He further says: 'As it was in the days of Noah, and in the days of Lot they did eat, they drank, they married wives, they bought, they sold, they planted, they built; even thus shall it be in the day when the Son of Man is revealed' (Luke 17:27-30). It is being made manifest that He is God and yet a man and not a spirit; for these things are now fulfilled as you and I see them that have eyes to see.[228]

**Luke 18:19 KJV-** And Jesus said unto him, Why callest thou me good? none is good, save one, that is, God.

---

[228] Muhammad, *Our Saviour Has Arrived*, 71-72.

**Luke 18:19 NIV-** "Why do you call me good?" Jesus answered. "No one is good—except God alone.

> **HEM-** Some of the Arab scholars say that the Holy One mentioned by Habakkuk (3:3) coming from Mount Paran refers to Muhammad- and they are right. But it does not refer to the Muhammad of the past but to the One Muhammad prophesied of in the Sunnah who came from His family in His name under the title, "Mahdi" (meaning the Guide, the Restorer of the Kingdom of Righteousness). This Holy One called "Mahdi" or Muhammad coming at the end of the world would come from the East out of the present Holy City, Mecca, Arabia, which is the East. This is the only holy place we know of that can produce a Holy One. Neither of the past two prophets, Jesus nor Muhammad, taught the people that they were Holy Ones, nor did they say that they were from heaven. Jesus himself denied that He was good; the only one good is God (St. Luke 18:19).[229]

**Luke 21:12 KJV-** But before all these, they shall lay their hands on you, and persecute you, delivering you up to the synagogues, and into prisons, being brought before kings and rulers for my name's sake.

**Luke 21:12 NIV-** But before all this, they will lay hands on you and persecute you. They will deliver you to synagogues and prisons, and you will be brought before kings and governors, and all on account of my name.

---

[229] Muhammad, *Our Saviour Has Arrived*, 71-72. see footnote 27 and 111.

> **HEM-** The prophecy of Jesus (Luke 21:12) of the sacrifice and trails to be made by the so-called Negroes could not be expressed in a clearer language: 'But before all these, they (the devils) shall lay their hands on you and persecute you delivering you (the Muslims) up to the synagogues (churches) and into prisons, being brought before kings and rulers for My name's sake.' It refers to none other than the so-called Negroes who accept their own religion, Islam, and a divine name from Allah. We are the hated ones in your midst and are persecuted for no other reason except that we are Muslims- under other charges such as our not joining on your side after truth and righteousness have come to us, and knowing God face to face as we know each other's faces.[230]

**Luke 21:25-26 KJV -** Men's hearts failing them for fear, and for looking after those things which are coming on the earth: for the powers of heaven shall be shaken. And then shall they see the Son of man coming in a cloud with power and great glory.

**Luke 21:25-26 NIV -** Men will faint from terror, apprehensive of what is coming on the world, for the heavenly bodies will be shaken. At that time they will see the Son of Man coming in a cloud with power and great glory.

> **HEM-** How true the prophecy of Jesus, Lu. 21:25-26 concerning the present time. We bear witness that the sea and waves are roaring and that fear is now covering the nations as shown by the unusual heart

---

[230] Muhammad, *Our Saviour Has Arrived*, 73.

failure that is now occurring among men. These are signs of the end of the present world. The sea and ocean are heaving up tidal waves to un-imaginable heights that man has never witnessed before on earth. This is another plague that is upon the wicked.[231]

**Luke 21:27 KJV-** And then shall they see the Son of man coming in a cloud with power and great glory.

**Luke 21:27 NIV-** At that time they will see the Son of Man coming in a cloud with power and great glory.

> **HEM-** I think I have made it clear to you that if we look forward to seeing or meeting God, He must be in the form of a man. The Christians' Bible bears me witness that God is a man of flesh and blood. The Bible predicts God coming as a man (Luke 21:27; Matthew 24:30; Revelation 1:7, 14:15). There is much proof in the Bible to support my claim that God is man. That is, if you want proof.[232]

---

[231] Muhammad, *The Fall of America*, 194.
[232] Muhammad, *Our Saviour Has Arrived*, 72.

# Chapter XXVII:

## John

**John 3:7 KJV-** Marvel not that I said unto thee, Ye must be born again.

**John 3:7 NIV-** You should not be surprised at my saying, "You must be born again."

> **HEM-** The world (of the white race) is doing what it was made to do- to try the righteous with wickedness and filth. The white race cannot do any better than what they are already doing. So we do not argue and quarrel with them, which they, by nature, are made to do. I repeatedly teach you this; that you cannot change the nature of the white man unless you graft him back into that which he was grafted out of. This is what Jesus means in the Bible, John 3:7 in his conversation with Nicodemus. He told him that in order to enter the kingdom of heaven he must be born again because in John 8:44 (Bible), Jesus had condemned all of the white race to be devils, and their father was the devil. There was no good nor truth in the father that made the white race.
> 
> So when a thing is what it is by the nature in which it was made or created in, you do not change it unless you go altogether back to the material that it (he) was made out of. So this demands a rebirth. Jesus was right - a rebirth - born again, all over. Some of the clergy and the scholars of Christianity take this to be a spiritual rebirth. But it means that the actual flesh and blood that was discussed in this conversation between Jesus and Nicodemus has to be changed. Then when

the man has been put back into what he was taken from, the spirit of that which he was put back into will come to him as the spirit to do evil comes to him now in what he is made in. For he was made out of evil. The white man was not made to obey Allah (God) and to seek after His Righteousness. So, therefore, to make the white man one of the righteous, the white man has to take on a new birth - the flesh and blood has to be changed.[233]

**John 4:22 KJV-** Ye worship ye know not what: we know what we worship: for salvation is of the Jews.

**John 4:22 NIV-** You Samaritans worship what you do not know; we worship what we do know, for salvation is from the Jews.

> **HEM-** The Divine Supreme Being. He is a Being which means that he exists and is not a spook. Christianity has blinded you to such worship as to worship that which you know not; as the Bible teaches you know not; (Bible, John 4:22). There has never been any change in the religion of Allah (God). It is their world's wickedness to deceive the Righteous that changes religion. The Pope of Rome is the father of such teachings as bringing in a religion other than the religion of Allah (God). The white race does not do the Will of our God; they were not made to do so. So do not think hard of them for not submitting to Allah (God) and for not believing in His religion, Islam. That is against their nature. However, some (few) of them here and there, throughout the world believe by faith. And now even the Pope of Rome's own preachers,

---

[233] Muhammad, *Our Saviour Has Arrived*, 77-78.

priests and cardinals are in the spirit of rebellion against Christianity because they know it is not true. Jesus was no author of Christianity. You cannot even prove it. The Pope of Rome will not try because he is wise. He knows what Jesus taught. It was Islam, as all the prophets before him taught. And how can we get around to believing in God if we do not believe in Islam after we learn that it is entire submission to the will of God.[234]

**John 4:23-24 KJV-** But the hour cometh, and now is, when the true worshippers shall worship the Father in spirit and in truth: for the Father seeketh such to worship him. God is a Spirit: and they that worship him must worship him in spirit and in truth.

**John 4:23-24 KJV-** Yet a time is coming and has now come when the true worshipers will worship the Father in spirit and truth, for they are the kind of worshipers the Father seeks. God is spirit, and his worshipers must worship in spirit and in truth.

> **HEM-** Many people have been saying for a long time that God is already with us. Most of the people believe God to be a "spirit". If He is only a spirit and not a man. The Bible teaches us of the spirit of God in many places; but only once do I find where it mentions God as being only a spirit (John 4:24). And this came from a Prophet (Jesus) and not from the mouth of God. If one reads the previous verse (John 4:23), he or she will see that even Jesus could not have believed God to be only a spirit in these words: 'But the hour cometh and now

---

[234] Muhammad, *Our Saviour Has Arrived,*192.

is when the true worshippers shall worship the Father in spirit and in truth; for the Father seeketh such to worship Him.' Here it is made clear that the 'hour cometh.' This doom or end of the devil's wicked world of false worshippers who claim that they are true worshippers of the true God but are not. For the Father (God) seeketh true worshippers. So Jesus could have only been referring to the time of the presence of God, in Person.[235]

**John 4:34 KJV-** Jesus saith unto them, My meat is to do the will of him that sent me, and to finish his work.

**John 4:34 NIV-** "My food," said Jesus, "is to do the will of him who sent me and to finish his work.

> **HEM-** If Jesus said that He was sent (Matt. 15:24 and John 4:34), then He cannot claim to be equal of His sender. God is not sent by anyone; He is a self-sender.[236]

**John 8:32 KJV-** And ye shall know the truth, and the truth shall make you free.

**John 8:32 NIV-** Then you will know the truth, and the truth will set you free.

> **HEM-** The misunderstanding of the Old and New Testaments by the so-called Negro preachers makes it our graveyard and must be resurrected there from. Moses didn't teach a resurrection of the dead nor did

---

[235] Muhammad, *Our Saviour Has Arrived*, 64-65.
[236] Muhammad, *Message to the Blackman in America*, 27.

Noah, who was a prophet before Moses. The New Testament and Holy Qur'an's teaching of a resurrection of the dead can't mean the people who have died physically and returned to the earth, but rather a mental resurrection of us, the black nation, who are mentally dead to the knowledge of truth; the truth of self, God and the arch-enemy of God and His people. That is the Truth (John 8:32) that will make us free, whereof John (8:32) doesn't say what truth shall make you free; therefore leaving it questionable and to the advantage of the enemy. "And ye shall know the truth, and the truth shall make you free."[237]

**HEM-** You, who have been here in America for four hundred years, have never been taught a true knowledge of self, God, and His religion, Islam. As long as you are without such essential knowledge, which is the key of salvation, freedom, justice, and equality, you are not free. It is true that the truth shall make the lost and found members of the Tribe of Shabazz (the so-called Negroes) free, (John 8:32) but they have never known what truth it was that shall make them free.[238]

**HEM-** If we shall know the truth (John 8:32) and that truth will make us free, we can truthfully say that we already have long since known the truth that Jesus was referring to was yet to come and not in his days (John 16:8, 13). If that truth had been revealed 2,000 years ago, there would not be any falsehood in the world. However, Jesus, being a prophet, foresaw the devil's rule. 'Seek the end of that which He (Yakub) has created.' The Father (Yakub) of the world created a

---

[237] Muhammad, *Message to the Blackman*, 96-97.
[238] Muhammad, *Our Saviour Has Arrived*, 20.

world of evil, discord, and hate. If you do not agree with their evil-doings, your goodness is the called hate or infidelity and you are called peace-breaker. [239]

**John 8:42 KJV-** Jesus said unto them, If God were your Father, ye would love me: for I proceeded forth and came from God; neither came I of myself, but he sent me.

**John 8:42 NIV-** Jesus said to them, "If God were your Father, you would love me, for I came from God and now am here. I have not come on my own; but he sent me.

> **HEM-** Read and study the above chapter of John 8:42, all of you, who are Christians, believers in the bible and Jesus, as you say. If you understand it right, you will agree with me that the whole Caucasian race is a race of devils. They have proved to be devils in the Garden of Paradise and were condemned 4,000 years later by Jesus. Likewise, they are condemned today, by the Great Mahdi Muhammad, as being nothing but devils in the plainest language. The so-called American Negroes have been deceived and blinded by their unlikeness, soft- smooth buttered words, eye-winking, back-patting, a false show of friendship and handshaking. The above mentioned acts, with the exception of handshaking, by men are a disgrace to any decent intelligent person. Know the truth and be free from such disgrace.[240]

**John 8:44 KJV-** Ye are of your father the devil, and the lusts of your father ye will do. He was a murderer from the beginning, and abode not in the truth, because there is no

---

[239] Muhammad, *Our Saviour Has Arrived*, 75-76.
[240] Muhammad, *Message to the Blackman* 23-24.

truth in him. When he speaketh a lie, he speaketh of his own: for he is a liar, and the father of it.

**John 8:44 NIV-** You belong to your father, the devil, and you want to carry out your father's desire. He was a murderer from the beginning, not holding to the truth, for there is no truth in him. When he lies, he speaks his native language, for he is a liar and the father of lies.

> **HEM-** Your letter is headed with 1 Thessalonians 3:14-16 and St. John 8:44-48. Why not 2 Thessalonians 2:3, 4, 7-12; also 1 Corinthians 10:21. All these as well as John 8:44 refer[s] to you and your race as the real devils, who even killed Jesus and the Prophets before Him, and who persecute us who believe and preach go to hell with you for believing and following you and your own Bible to pick that which condemns your own self! I am real happy to have received such open confessions of your evil self, as I am doing all I can to make the Negroes see that you and your religion are their open enemies, and to prove to them that they will never be anything but your slaves and finally go to hell with you for believing and following you and your kind.[241]

> **HEM-** The white race was made by nature without the truth. Jesus said (Bible John 8:44) that there was no truth in them, for their father was a liar and a murderer. Therefore his children (white race) cannot be otherwise. We should know the seriousness of the

---

[241] Muhammad, *Message to the Blackman*, 338-339. See entire letter from to J.B. Stoner, Arch Leader of the Christian Knights of The Ku Klux Klan, and response from the Most Hon. Elijah Muhammad (*Message to the Blackman in America*. 330-341).

time that we are now living in. The truth will save our lives if we believe it.[242]

**HEM-** Yakub, the father of the devil, made the white race, a race of devils – enemies of the darker people of the earth. The white race is not made by nature to accept righteousness. They know righteousness, but they cannot be righteous. Jesus made this clear when he was trying to reform the white race (devils) two thousand (2,000) years ago (Bible, Jn. 8:44). If you and I believe that the devils are from the God of Righteousness, we are making the God of Righteousness an evil god, who created an evil god, and made the evil god to become the best guide for the people of righteousness. The God of Righteousness Would Not Make an enemy of righteousness as the best guide for keeping the righteous people on the right path. Allah (God) Master Fard Muhammad, to Whom Praises are due forever, Comes in Person, to teach us the right way and to point out to us the great arch deceiver (white race, devils). That the white race is a race of devils is the most hated truth that they are opposing in the last days (resurrection of the mentally dead).[243]

**HEM-** The Black man has been ruled under falsehood by a false teacher (devil). His teachings are false because he did not teach the people truth. The devil himself, was not made out of truth; he was made out of falsehood (Bible Jn. 8:44). Therefore, the Black People who follow the white man (their made enemy) are not following truth; they are following falsehood. The religion of the white man (Christianity) is falsehood.

---

[242] Muhammad, *Our Saviour Has Arrived*, 11.
[243] Ibid., 90

The white man adds falsehood to the truth and mixes truth with falsehood. Formerly this blinded the eyes of the man who had lost the knowledge of himself (Black man of America).[244]

**John 13:34 KJV-** A new commandment I give unto you, That ye love one another; as I have loved you, that ye also love one another.

**John 13:34 NIV-** A new command I give you: Love one another. As I have loved you, so you must love one another.

> **HEM-** The prophet (Eze. 47:12, Bible) says that Allah (God) will even make new trees and shall bring forth new fruit. Jn. 13:34 prophesies that a new commandment shall be given to us which will make you able ministers of a new testament. 2 Cor. 3:6 and 2 Cor. 5:17 says that 'if any man be in Christ, he is a new creature.' Eph. 2:15, prophesies 'of twain, one new man, so making peace.' The Bible, 2 Pet. 3:13, prophesies, 'We look for new heaven and a new earth' and Rev. 21:5, 'He said, behold, I make all things new.' Since the Bible here has promised through the mouth of the prophets, that Allah (God) Raised Up in Israel will be brought about when the God of the Resurrection of the Dead Appears, the Dead will no more be as they once were. They will become new creatures.[245]

**John 15:17 KJV-** These things I command you, that ye love one another.

---

[244] Muhammad, *Our Saviour Has Arrived*, 201.
[245] Ibid.,114.

**John 15:17 NIV-** This is my command: Love each other.

> **HEM-** "You say of yourself, "I love everybody." This cannot be true. Love for self comes first. The Bible, the book that you claim to believe says, "Love the brotherhood" (I Peter 2:17). "Love one another" (John 15:17). Love of self comes first. The one who loves everybody is the one who does not love anyone. This is the false teaching of the Christians for the Christians war against Christians. They have the Bible so twisted by adding in and taking out of the truth that it takes only God or one whom God has given the knowledge of the Book to understand it.[246]

**John 17:9 KJV-** I pray for them: I pray not for the world, but for them which thou hast given me; for they are thine.

**John 17:9 NIV-** I pray for them. I am not praying for the world, but for those you have given me, for they are yours.

> **HEM-** The worst blind teaching that is going on is from Black preachers trying to prove that Jesus is the Son of God and that he died to save the world. This is carrying the Black Man to hell faster than anything that you can teach him; that Jesus died to save the world. This is an addition where the translators did not make it clear whose world the God will save. It was not the world of the enemies of God. This world is destined to be destroyed according to Jesus' prophecy and all the prophets before him. The Black Man does not belong to this world. The only Black Men who belong to this world are those who make themselves belong to this

---

[246] Muhammad, *Message to the Blackman in America*, 33.

world. You must remember that the white man's world is a distinct world of his own. He is the god of this world until today when he meets the right Owner, The Great God, Allah. The Jesus says (Bible, John 17:9) that he did not even pray for the world; that he prayed to God to take care of those whom he had converted out of the world. He did not come to the God, praying to Him to save the world. And, again in the Bible, it is written that a sinner's prayer is not even heard. And the real sinner is the devil.[247]

**HEM-** The gravest mistake that the Black Man is making today is his trying to hold on to the belief in the return of Jesus or that he lived and preached the saving of the white man's world. This is false. Jesus did not preach this. See Bible, Jn. 17:9. Jesus had a few disciples. Jesus also cursed the Jews, not to mention that he was trying to save them...or the Caucasian people.[248]

**HEM-** And what right do you have to preach that he died for the world when he said he did not even pray for the world for you who are in love with the world that he was not in love with. He condemned the world as being a world of devils (Bible, John 8:44) and said that they were the prince of this world (Bible, John 12:31, Mt. 4:9). So the white race is not the universal ruler as god, but they were to rule for the time that they were given to rule. They were given power and wisdom to rule as god of their own world; and that is the civilization of the white race has conquered the air as well as the sea and land because they have gotten out of the rotation of the earth. This means they have

---

[247] Muhammad, *Our Saviour Has Arrived*, 193.
[248] Muhammad, *The Fall of America*, 214.

conquered the atmosphere of the earth and have gone into airless space. Oh, foolish Brothers, you certainly do not know the scriptures and you are too proud to be taught. While your Bible teaches you (James 4:4) that he who loves this world is at enmity with God, the blind preachers are leading the Black people to hell as the Bible teaches; they all went in the Lake of Fire with their followers, believing in the devil (Rev. 19:20). As Jesus was not of the world of the white man, so are we of the world of the white man. And the parable that he put before you prophesies how God would come, searching for you to take you out of the world of the wicked, and put you into your own world of Peace and security. Also see Bible (Ez. 34, Bible). As Jesus prophesied of the Black preacher (Mt. 23:13, Bible), you will not come into the kingdom of Heaven (the religion of Islam), nor will you suffer those who are trying to come in. This is a bad scripture on the Black preacher. But you are so blind that you do not know that it is talking about you, but it is you, and not the Jews. (No. 2 Th. 2:3) says that you will not come until the man of sin was revealed. [249]

---

[249]Muhammad, *Our Saviour Has Arrived*, 193-94.

# Chapter XXVIII:

## I John

**I John 5:19 KJV-** And we know that we are of God, and the whole world lieth in wickedness.

**I John 5:19 NIV-** We know that we are children of God, and that the whole world is under the control of the evil one.

> **HEM-** Ever since Adam, the Caucasian race has been referred to as the man-made man or race and mankind; the world has taken this to include all men. 'No man hath seen God.' (I John 5:19). This is another confused teaching to the ignorant masses; for if no man hath seen God, then there is no God for you and me to look forward to seeing on the Judgment Day. The whole world of the white race is full of wickedness and this is the 'world' referred to. We are not of this 'world' (the white race or devils) nor is our God the God of this world of devil.[250]

---

[250] Muhammad, *Our Saviour Has Arrived*, 66-67.

# Chapter XXIX:

## I Corinthians

**I Corinthians 10:21 KJV-** Ye cannot drink the cup of the Lord, and the cup of devils: ye cannot be partakers of the Lord's table, and of the table of devils.

**I Corinthians 10:21 NIV-** You cannot drink the cup of the Lord and the cup of demons too; you cannot have a part in both the Lord's table and the table of demons.

> **HEM-** The Bible warns us against the love and worship of these devils. Psalms 106:37, says "Yea, they sacrificed their sons and their daughters unto devils."
> In another place it states, "And I would not that you should have fellowship with devils. Ye cannot drink the cup of the Lord, and the cup of the devils: ye cannot be partakers of the Lord's table and of the table of the devils. (1 Cor. 10:-21). "They should not worship up devils" (Rev. 9:20). The so-called Negroes, because of their fear and ignorance of this real open enemy devil, will fall victim to them if we do not constantly warn them of the consequences. I am willing to die for the so-called Negro that they may see and understand the truth of self, God and this race of devils. We have served them well through ignorance and blindness because of being without a teacher. Allah (God) has given you one. I, Elijah Muhammad am from God, Himself! Why not believe and follow me? Are you afraid of being persecuted for the sake of truth to this

> 22 million blind, deaf, and dumb lost-found Nation of Islam? In that case, you life is already doomed.[251]
>
> **HEM-** They, the white race, cannot treat you and me with justice and equality. They cannot do so among themselves. Even though they are against us. This does not mean that they have love and peace for each other. No! They war against each other all the time. They are devils. No heart of love and mercy are in them as you may think. Nature did not give them such a heart.[252]

**I Corinthians 15:50 KJV-** Now this I say, brethren, that flesh and blood cannot inherit the kingdom of God; neither doth corruption inherit incorruption.

**I Corinthians 15:50 NIV-** I declare to you, brothers, that flesh and blood cannot inherit the kingdom of God, nor does the perishable inherit the imperishable.

> **HEM-** My friends use a bit of common sense. First, could a wonderful flesh and blood body, made of the essence of our earth, last 2,000 years on the earth, or off the earth, without being healed! Second, where exists such a heaven, of the earth, that flesh and blood of the earth can exist, since the Bible teaches that flesh and blood cannot enter heaven? (Cor. 15:50) Flesh and blood cannot survive without that of which it is made, the earth. Jesus' prophesy of the coming of the Son of Man is very clear, if you rightly understand. First, this removes all doubt about who we should expect to execute judgment, for if man is to be judged and rewarded according to his actions, who could be

---

[251] Muhammad, *Message to the Blackman in America*, 232.
[252] Ibid., 231-232.

justified in sitting as judge of man's doings but another man? How could a spirit be our judge when we cannot see a spirit? And ever since life was created, life has had spirit. But the Bible teaches that God will be seen on the Day of Judgment. Not only the righteous will see Him, but even His enemies shall see Him.[253]

---

[253] Muhammad, *Message to the Blackman in America*, 12.

# Chapter XXX:

## II Corinthians

**II Corinthians 5:17 KJV-** Therefore if any man be in Christ, he is a new creature: old things are passed away; behold, all things are become new.

**II Corinthians 5:17 NIV-** Therefore, if anyone is in Christ, he is a new creation; the old has gone, the new has come!

> **HEM-** The Bible, 2 Cor. 5:17 says 'Therefore if any man be in Christ, he is a new creature; old things are passed away: behold, all things are become new.' 'All who are in Christ is a new creature.' This Christ Who is referred to in the above verse is Allah (God) in Person (The Mahdi). This is true and the scriptures prophecy teaches you that You have to be new to be one of His followers. He changes you in mind; and it is written 'as man think, so is he' (Pr. 23:7). Christ the true interpretation of the Name is 'The Crusher.' When understood, it makes the God Coming in the Last Day to Crush the wicked to be the True Answer to that Name of Christ. You call Him the Anointed One That is true. He is Anointed to Crush the wicked. He does Not Come loving the wicked as you would like Him to do since you are wicked yourself.[254]

---

[254] Muhammad, *Our Saviour Has Arrived,* 128-29.

# Chapter XXXI:

## II Thessalonians

**II Thessalonians 2:3-12 KJV-** Let no man deceive you by any means: for that day shall not come, except there come a falling away first, and that man of sin be revealed, the son of perdition; Who opposeth and exalteth himself above all that is called God, or that is worshipped; so that he as God sitteth in the temple of God, shewing himself that he is God. Remember ye not, that, when I was yet with you, I told you these things? And now ye know what withholdeth that he might be revealed in his time. For the mystery of iniquity doth already work: only he who now letteth will let, until he be taken out of the way. And then shall that Wicked be revealed, whom the Lord shall consume with the spirit of his mouth, and shall destroy with the brightness of his coming: Even him, whose coming is after the working of Satan with all power and signs and lying wonders, And with all deceivableness of unrighteousness in them that perish; because they received not the love of the truth, that they might be saved. And for this cause God shall send them strong delusion, that they should believe a lie: That they all might be damned who believed not the truth, but had pleasure in unrighteousness.

**II Thessalonians 2:3-12 NIV-** Don't let anyone deceive you in any way, for (that day will not come) until the rebellion occurs and the man of lawlessness is revealed, the man doomed to destruction. [4]He will oppose and will exalt himself over everything that is called God or is worshiped, so that he sets himself up in God's temple, proclaiming himself to be God. Don't you remember that when I was with you I used to tell you these things? And now you know what is holding him back, so that he may be revealed at the proper time. For the secret power of lawlessness is already at work; but the one who now holds it back will continue to do so till he is taken out of the way. And then the lawless one will be revealed, whom the Lord Jesus will overthrow with the breath of his mouth and destroy by the splendor of his coming. The coming of the lawless one will be in accordance with the work of Satan displayed in all kinds of counterfeit miracles, signs and wonders, and in every sort of evil that deceives those who are perishing. They perish because they refused to love the truth and so be saved. For this reason God sends them a powerful delusion so that they will believe the lie and so that all will be condemned who have not believed the truth but have delighted in wickedness.

> **HEM-** Remember the Bible's teaching of this race of devils, and especially II Thessalonians (Chapter 2:3-12), and Revelation (12:9-17,20:10). The treatment of the so-called Negroes by the devils is sufficient proof to the so-called Negroes, that they (the white race), are real devils. And if this teaching, along with what they are suffering from their beloved devils, does not awaken them to the knowledge of the devils, all I can say for them, then is that they are just lost. They won't be accepted by God nor by the righteous Muslims, with even the name of the devils. Muhammad took hold of the best, the belief in one God (Allah), and was successful. Fourteen hundred years after him we are successful. That is, we who will not set up another God with Allah. The fools who refuse to believe in Allah

alone, as the one God, if asked: Who made the heavens and earth? Most surely would say God, and would not say: God, the Son, and the Holy Ghost. Then why don't they serve and obey Allah?[255]

**HEM-** According to Allah, the origin of such teachings as a Mystery God is from the devils! It was taught to them by their father, Yakub, 6,000 years ago. They know today that God is not a mystery but will not teach it. He (devil), the god of evil, was made to rule the nations of earth for 6,000 years, and naturally he would not teach obedience to a God other than himself. So, a knowledge of the true God of Righteousness was not represented by the devils. The true God was not to be made manifest to the people until the god of evil (devil) has finished or lived out his time, which was allowed to deceive the nations (read These. 2:9-10, Rev. 20:3-10).[256]

**HEM-** God must fulfill His promise to show Himself as God over all the powers of heaven and earth, and men on earth. As it is written (Thessalonians 2:9), "He comes after the workings of Satan." Satan has been given the power, knowledge and authority to deceive as many as he could before the appearance of God or the universal manifestation of the presence of God. He was given this power in the beginning, according to Chapter 2 and 7 of the Holy Qur'an, and according to the Bible in Genesis 1:26, Revelations 6:4,8, and Revelations 12:3,4.[257]

---

[255] Muhammad, *Message to the Blackman*, 106.
[256] Ibid., 2
[257] Muhammad, *The Fall of America*, 190-91.

**II Thessalonians 3:16 KJV-** Now the Lord of peace himself give you peace always by all means. The Lord be with you all.

**II Thessalonians 3:16 NIV-** Now may the Lord of peace himself give you peace at all times and in every way. The Lord be with all of you.

> **HEM-** The significance of the name "Islam" is peace, the true religion. It is a religion of eternal peace. We cannot imagine Allah (God) offering to us a religion other than one of peace. A religion of peace coming to the righteous after the destruction of the wicked is also mentioned in several places in the Bible: "The Lord will bless His people with peace." (Psa. 29:11): also, "He will speak peace unto His people and to His saints" (Psa. 35:8) and "the Lord of Peace give you peace always" (II Thess. 3:16). Islam is the religion referred to in the above-mentioned Biblical verses.[258]

---

[258] Muhammad, *Message to the Blackman in America*, 69-70.

# Chapter XXXII:

## James

**James 4:4-6 KJV-** Ye adulterers and adulteresses, know ye not that the friendship of the world is enmity with God? whosoever therefore will be a friend of the world is the enemy of God. Do ye think that the scripture saith in vain, The spirit that dwelleth in us lusteth to envy? But he giveth more grace. Wherefore he saith, God resisteth the proud, but giveth grace unto the humble.

**James 4:4-6 NIV-** You adulterous people, don't you know that friendship with the world is hatred toward God? Anyone who chooses to be a friend of the world becomes an enemy of God. Or do you think Scripture says without reason that the spirit he caused to live in us envies intensely? He gives us more grace. That is why Scripture says: God opposes the proud but gives grace to the humble.

> **HEM-** The Bible warns them against the friendship of the devils (James 4:4). "Whosoever therefore will be a friend of the world is the enemy of God." The sixth verse of the same chapter reads: "Submit yourselves therefore to God. Resist the devil, and he will flee from you." Do they resist the devils? No! Being without the truth of Allah and the devil, they are afraid; and that fear is the cause of their suffering and will be the cause of their destruction in hell, with the devils whom they love and fear. [259]

---

[259] Muhammad, *Message to the Blackman in America*, 109.

**James 5:6 KJV-** Ye have condemned and killed the just; and he doth not resist you.

**James 5:6 NIV-** You have condemned and murdered innocent men, who were not opposing you.

> **HEM-** That awful day of yours will surely come -- the appointed hour you are hasting by your evil intentions and doings to us, the poor black people. We who have given our sweat and blood all our lives today we cry for justice and you send your armed forces with trained wild dogs to kill us as it is written of you. "Ye have condemned and killed the just, and he doth not resist you" (James 5:6). You send armies of heavily armed policemen to slay the unarmed so-called Negroes. Does this act of murder of unarmed people show that you are brave or cowards? You, like your fathers, hate and despise your slaves, and you beat and murder them daily. And after such inhuman treatment you want them to love you so that you may carry out your evil doings on them without resistance.
>
> The beating and killing of those among us who say they are Muslims is most surely hasting your doom. You hate them because Allah has revealed the truth of you to them and you are angry and seek to take revenge on them for what Allah has made known to them of truth. There is no solution to the problem between the slave-masters and their slaves other than the once slaves are going for self, for they have become a nation in a nation. One or the other must leave the other or suffer death. [260]

---

[260] Muhammad, *Message to the Blackman in America*, 258-59.

We, the Muslims, have tried to live in peace here in America. There is not a single incident in our thirty-six years of history where we have ever made an aggressive move against you, but you have attacked us several times. We have proved to the world that you are impossible to live with in peace. "Ye have condemned and killed the just and he doth not resist you." (James 5:6) You have destroyed many towns, cities and people. As thou have divided the so-called Negro, one against the other, so Allah shall divide you and your brethren.[261]

---

[261] Muhammad, *The Fall of America*, 167.

# Chapter XXXIII:

## I Peter

**I Peter 2:17 KJV-** Honour all men. Love the brotherhood. Fear God. Honour the king.

**I Peter 2:17 NIV-** Show proper respect to everyone: Love the brotherhood of believers, fear God, honor the king.

> **HEM-** You say of yourself, "I love everybody." This cannot be true. Love for self comes first. The Bible, the book that you claim to believe says, "Love the brotherhood" (I Peter 2:17). "Love one another" (John 15:17). Love of self comes first. The one who loves everybody is the one who does not love anyone. This is the false teaching of the Christians for the Christians war against Christians. They have the Bible so twisted by adding in and taking out of the truth that it takes only God or one whom God has given the knowledge of the Book to understand it.[262]

---

[262] Muhammad, *Message to the Blackman in America*,.33.

# Chapter XXXIV:

## II Peter

**II Peter 3:10 KJV-** But the day of the Lord will come as a thief in the night; in the which the heavens shall pass away with a great noise, and the elements shall melt with fervent heat, the earth also and the works that are therein shall be burned up.

**II Peter 3:10 NIV-** But the day of the Lord will come like a thief. The heavens will disappear with a roar; the elements will be destroyed by fire, and the earth and everything in it will be laid bare.

> **HEM-** The extent to which the enemy has poisoned the minds and hearts of my people here in America is shameful. They willfully do anything to deceive the so-called Negroes into going to their doom with them. There is no way for the enemy of Allah, His Messenger and His people (the darker people of the earth) to find strength, power and wisdom enough to win in a war against Allah. As it is written in the Christian Bible and many other places: "But the day of the Lord will come as a thief in the night; in thee, which the heavens shall pass away with a great noise and the elements shall melt with fervent heat, the earth also and the works that are therein shall be burned up" (Peter 3:10). The earth shall not be burned; it will be here for many thousands of years to come. Only that on the earth (the devils) which has sinned against Allah and His laws will be destroyed. The earth, the sun, the moon and the

stars have never disobeyed Allah since their creation.[263]

**HEM-** Come Follow Me, I say. I will lead you to your God of Salvation. If you stay where you are, you will suffer the consequences. Just as a reminder, read the Bible Jer. 50:46 and II Pet. 3:10. It is terrible, awful, and frightful; to look up and instead of seeing a blue sky, see a sky of flames and fire. This will surely come. Allah (God) has affirmed this prophecy with me. The whole heavens will be blotted out and in its place there will be a canopy of flame. The heavens and elements that make up the atmosphere of the earth will melt with fervent heat. There will be an explosion of the total atmosphere of the earth by God Himself. Take Heed of it, for the Holy Qur'an says such a time as we are entering into now is a grievous time. It will make children's hair turn gray. If the grief and excitement will make children turn gray because of the terribleness of judgment, what do you think our hair will be doing? The Bible prophesies gray and baldness upon all heads. My people stop thinking of sport and play and think over your life and the safety of your life.[264]

---

[263] Muhammad, *Message to the Blackman in America*, 280-81. Muhammad, *The Fall of America*, 45-46.
[264] Muhammad, *Our Saviour Has Arrived*, 105-06.

# Chapter XXXV:

## Revelation

**HEM-** The nations of the earth are becoming her enemies because of the evils and the murders of the so-called American Negroes, who now could choose to build the kingdom of heaven. There is no let- up in her evil, brutality and murder of her once slaves (the Negro) who are still her slaves mentally. She would not like you to know that the doom is because of the way she treated her slaves. She has deceived everyone who deals with her, as recorded in the Revelations of John of the Bible. Today, she has, as the Revelation of John prophesied, the head of the church (the Pope of Rome) helping her deceive Negroes and keep them in the church so that they may be destroyed with her. The only thing that will hold the Negro is his belief in whites as a people of divinity. They hold to his religion (Christianity) which they use to deceive everyone they possibly can. It was through Christianity that they got their authority over the black, brown, yellow and red races.[265]

**HEM-** The Revelation of John in the Bible (the Revelator represents them spiritually as beasts because of their savage way of dealing with and murdering black people) and even Isaiah warn you who hold to the white man's names and his religion. This is your America. We have proven this to you, not your slave-master that you will get respect and honor throughout the world if you accept your own and take on the

---

[265] Muhammad, *Message to the Blackman in America*, 47.

names of the divine Supreme Being. It is in your Bible, and now it has been made manifest to you.[266]

**HEM-** Would you like to say to the prophets who prophesied (and their prophecies are written) that they lied when they said that this world of evil had a limit of time six thousand (6,000) years? The six (6) workdays in their work-week are to remind them of their eventual end. "Six (6) days (6,000 years) thou shalt do all of thy work and on the seventh (7th) day thou shalt rest (die). And all of thy work shall be destroyed and thy name shalt be destroyed that this race be no more remembered among the Nations of the Righteous."

Do you think all of this is false prophecy just because you love evil and hate good? This is not the first time that a new change has come into effect among the people. Take, for instance, their six thousand (6,000) years are divided into two's (2's). Also at the beginning of our (Black Man's) Creation, it is divided into two's (2's) and ends in the number six (6). This is the reason that in the Book of Revelations the Bible teaches us that the enemy's number is the same as the number of the Black Man. The enemy has a number of six (6), but the difference between his number six (6) and our (the Black Man's) number six (6) is that the enemy's time of rule is of short duration while we (Black Man) can look proudly to infinity of time in our history.[267]

**HEM-** In the Bible, John in The Revelation sees the preachers and his followers burning in hell fire with the devil, the white slave masters. I do not care how much you teach or tell the "reverend" that he is headed

---

[266] Muhammad, *Message to the Blackman in America*, 47-48.
[267] Muhammad, *Our Saviour Has Arrived*, 118-19.

for hell in following the white slave-master, devil; they ignore the warning for the sake of the honor of the white slave master. But when you look into it, you will see that the white slave master is not honoring the "reverend;" he is fooling him. The white slave master cares nothing about the "reverend" that he has made, and he thinks that the "reverend" is a fool for following him. It is written in the Bible which teaches the "reverend" against following the devil. The people who work as the devil's disciples are called "reverend." The word "reverend" means "to respect" but this is a false honor from the devil and yet the reverend goes still and he will walk right into the lake of hellfire with the devil, as long as the devil calls him "reverend" or "father."[268]

**Revelation 1:7 KJV-** Behold, he cometh with clouds; and every eye shall see him, and they also which pierced him: and all kindreds of the earth shall wail because of him. Even so, Amen.

**Revelation 1:7 NIV-** Look, he is coming with the clouds, and every eye will see him, even those who pierced him; and all the peoples of the earth will mourn because of him. So shall it be! Amen.

> **HEM-** You have been taught so long that God is not a man, so you have become hardened against believing in anything other than what you have been taught. "Every eye shall see Him." (Rev. 1:7). No eye can see spirits. The above chapter says: 'All kindreds of the earth shall wail (shall be sorry to see His coming)

---

[268] Muhammad, *The Fall of America*, 21.

because of Him.' Never was this so true as it is today.²⁶⁹

**HEM-** Master Fard Muhammad, to Whom Praises are Due forever is The All Wise and Living God. He Desires that we see Him as He is a Human Being and not something beyond the family of human beings...spookisms. We could never ask a formless spirit to lead us because we are not a formless spirit ourselves. Man can only listen to man. Man cannot listen to other than man. And I have proof. We just never were able to obey anything but ourselves! We, the once Dead, mentally, are coming to the knowledge of life; when we learn this lesson of the living, it will destroy the belief in other than ourselves.

Bringing us up in slavery time putting us to a mental death was something that the slave master and his children did because of their desire to make us into something that was other than the truth, in order to be able to keep our minds enslaved! From the Visit of God, in the Person of Master Fare Muhammad to Whom Praises are Due forever, the Time, now, has come to us, as it is written. That on the Day of Judgment, we will see God as He Is (Bible; Rev. 1:7.).²⁷⁰

**Revelation 1:14 KJV-** His head and his hairs were white like wool, as white as snow; and his eyes were as a flame of fire.

**Revelation 1:14 NIV-** His head and hair were white like wool, as white as snow, and his eyes were like blazing fire.

---

[269] Muhammad, *Our Saviour Has Arrived*, 72.
[270] Muhammad, *The Fall of America*, 38-39.

> **HEM-** We must do our utmost to keep our nation pure by keeping the white race away from our women. We're proud of our Black skin and our kinky wool; for this kinky wool hair is that of the future ruler. Look into your poison book, Dan. 7:9, Rev. 1:14. It has been boasted that America is a white man's country, but why did they bring us here? If the white race is such a super race, why don't they live alone and leave us to live alone in our own country? Why are they fighting to stay in Asia? Why not be satisfied with Europe and America? We didn't ask to be brought here.[271]

**Revelation 7:3 KJV-** Saying, Hurt not the earth, neither the sea, nor the trees, till we have sealed the servants of our God in their foreheads.

**Revelation 7:3 NIV-** Do not harm the land or the sea or the trees until we put a seal on the foreheads of the servants of our God.

> **HEM-** His Name of Praise and of 'worthy of Praise' are just a few of the Great Names Which Belong to God, and He Wants to Give Them to us. The Bible teaches us that He Will Give His Names to those who believe in Him. According to the Bible, Rev. 7:3, the Judgment cannot take place until those Who Believe in Him are Given His Name (sealed in their forehead). [272]

**Revelation 9:6 KJV-** And in those days shall men seek death, and shall not find it; and shall desire to die, and death shall flee from them.

---

[271] See Daniel 7:9.
[272] Muhammad, *Our Saviour Has Arrived*, 102.

**Revelation 9:6 KJV-** During those days men will seek death, but will not find it; they will long to die, but death will elude them.

> **HEM-** The consequence of this rejection of His call will get you a disgraceful year=s punishment or chastisement (night and day). You will wish that you were dead. When night comes, you will wish it were day, and when day comes, you will wish it night. You can find this chastisement mentioned in Revelation (Rev. 9:6; 19:20; 20:10, 14, 15, and 21:8). Salvation has come to the black men of America, but their fear of losing the hate -- I cannot say the love because they do not love you -- of their enemies causes them to reject it. Within 24 months, every one of you who is now a disbeliever in Allah and the great brotherhood of Islam will be suffering the punishments that have been mentioned in the above chapters and verses. America is the first country and people that Allah wishes to destroy, but he will not destroy them until you have heard the truth of her and of yourself. I shall continue to warn you of the divine penalty that awaits you who reject your God and my Saviour, Master Fard Muhammad. In this world of crisis and destruction of nations, the only escape you have is in Allah and following me.[273]

**Revelation 11:18 KJV-** And the nations were angry, and thy wrath is come, and the time of the dead, that they should be judged, and that thou shouldest give reward unto thy servants the prophets, and to the saints, and them

---

[273] Muhammad, *Message to the Blackman*, 297-98. Also see pg.232. See Psalms 106:37, 1 Corinthians 10:21 for further explanation of Revelation 9:6.

that fear thy name, small and great; and shouldest destroy them which destroy the earth.

**Revelation 11:18 NIV-** The nations were angry; and your wrath has come. The time has come for judging the dead and for rewarding your servants the prophets and your saints and those who reverence your name, both small and great and for destroying those who destroy the earth.

> **HEM-** They are mad and cannot see, nor hear the truth. So they call the truth false and the false they call truth. The truth (Islam) has angered them (Christianity). 'And the nations (Christianity) were angry. Thy wrath is come. The time of the dead (The mentally dead Black nation- especially the so-called Negro, must come into the knowledge of the truth of their enemies and the enemies' false religion that was used to deceive them. They shall give reward unto Thy servants, the prophets, and the saints, and will destroy them which destroy the earth' (Bible, Rev. 11:18).[274]

## Revelation 12

> **HEM-** Rev. Ch. 12 (Bible) prophesies of America under the worst names that could be given to a human being: serpent, snake, Satan, devil, and the deceiver of the people of the earth.[275]

**Revelation 12:4 KJV-** And his tail drew the third part of the stars of heaven, and did cast them to the earth: and the

---

[274] Muhammad, *Our Saviour Has Arrived*, 76.
[275] Muhammad, *The Fall of America*, 108.

dragon stood before the woman which was ready to be delivered, for to devour her child as soon as it was born.

**Revelation 12:4 NIV-** His tail swept a third of the stars out of the sky and flung them to the earth. The dragon stood in front of the woman who was about to give birth, so that he might devour her child the moment it was born.

> **HEM-** The serpent, the devil, dragon, Satan, seems to have been seeking the weaker part of man (the woman) to bring to naught the man- the Divine Man. It is his first and last trick to deceive the people of God through the woman or with the woman. He is using his woman to tempt the black man by parading her half-nude before his eyes and with public love-making, indecent kissing and dancing over radio and television screens and throughout their public papers and magazines. He is flooding the world with propaganda against God and His true religion, Islam. He stands before the so-called Negro woman to deceive her by feigning love and love-making with her, give the so-called Negro woman preference over her husband or brother in hiring. ...The woman in Rev 12:4 actually refers to the last Apostle of God, and her child refers to his followers, or the entire Negro race as they are called, who are not ready to be delivered (go to their own).[276]

> **HEM-** Take this anger and dislike on the part of the beast that seeks to destroy the child of a woman, Bible, Rev. 12:4 and the dragon stood before the woman which was ready to be delivered, for to devour her child as soon as it was born.' If Mary and her son are a

---

[276] Muhammad, *Message to the Blackman*, 127.

sign, or an example, of that which is to come, then whose birth and enslavement could correspond with these prophecies and signs any more than we, the American So-Called Negroes here under the white man?[277]

**HEM-** The arch deceivers force war against themselves. Their ultimate aim is to do as their people always have done -- try to destroy the preacher of truth and those who believe and follow him. This was the aim of Cain when he slew his brother, Abel, and the aim of the dragon when he sought to destroy the woman (the Messenger), as it is written in Revelations 12:4.[278]

**Revelation 12:9 KJV-** And the great dragon was cast out, that old serpent, called the Devil, and Satan, which deceiveth the whole world: he was cast out into the earth, and his angels were cast out with him.

**Revelation 12:9 NIV-** The great dragon was hurled down—that ancient serpent called the devil, or Satan, who leads the whole world astray. He was hurled to the earth, and his angels with him.

**HEM-** We know that there was never a time when an actual serpent (or snake) could talk and deceive people in the knowledge of God's law. This same serpent is mentioned in Revelation 12:9 as a deceiver. There (12:9) it is made clear to us that the serpent is "the

---

[277] Muhammad, *Our Saviour Has Arrived*, 161. See also Thessalonians 2.9.
[278] Muhammad, *The Fall of America*, 189-90.

dragon, devil and Satan which deceiveth the whole world."[279]

**HEM-** That old serpent, called the devil and Satan, which deceiveth the whole world (Rev. 12:9) is a person or persons whose characteristics are like that of a serpent (snake). Serpents or snakes of the grafted type cannot be trusted, for they will strike you when you are not expecting a strike.[280]

**HEM-** Remember the Bible's teaching of this race of devils, and especially in II Thessalonians (Chapter 2:3-12), and Revelation (12:9-17, 20:10). The treatment of the so-called Negroes by the devils is sufficient proof to the so-called Negroes, that they (the white race,) are real devils.[281]

**HEM-** As you know, the Revelation of the Bible under the title of John teaches us that the old dragon beast (referring to the white civilization) deceived the whole world, and they have done just that. Allah has taught me they deceived 90 percent of the planet earth. The only way the white race can survive and rule is by making false appear as truth and truth to appear as false.[282]

**HEM-** The devil (white man) will deceive many of you (Bible Rev. 12:9) with his soft buttered words and his love songs and with his promises to you that he never intends to fulfill (Holy Qur'an 4:120). It is written of him that he will deceive you in this way. But by

---

[279] Muhammad, *Message to the Blackman*, 127.
[280] Ibid.
[281] Muhammad, *Our Saviour Has Arrived*, 106.
[282] Ibid., 10-11

having a thorough knowledge of the arch deceiver, you should not fall victim of his deceitful teaching and love-making. Any sane man who knows fire and its burn is not going to put his hand in it. So when you know these things a surety, with experience, you should not be partakers of it.[283]

**HEM-** The lost-found members of that nation should be taught to know the ultimate aim of this world. God has visited them, and has prepared a teacher (in myself) to teach them, thereby making it easy for them to understand and recognize this world and its secret, ultimate aim. It is even given in the Bible, in Revelations 12:9. There it speaks of the members belonging to the righteous nation, and shows that through deceit, Satan causes them to become as himself against the truth, peace, justice, safety and security one would enjoy if he only were not deceived.[284]

**Revelation 12:12-13 KJV-** Therefore rejoice ye heavens, and ye that dwell in them. Woe to the inhabiters of the earth and of the sea! For the devil is come down unto you, having great wrath, because he knoweth that he hath but a short time. And when the dragon saw that he was cast unto the earth, he persecuted the woman which brought forth the man child.

**Revelation 12:12-13 NIV-** Therefore rejoice you heavens and you who dwell in them! But woe to the earth and the sea, because the devil has gone down to you! He is filled with fury, because he knows that his time is short." When

---

[283] Muhammad, *Our Saviour Has Arrived*, 202.
[284] Muhammad, *The Fall of America*, 190.

the dragon saw that he had been hurled to the earth, he pursued the woman who had given birth to the male child.

> **HEM-** The wicked world of the white race today actually does not want a God of Righteousness to set up a government of justice and righteousness, for they love what they have- wickedness, sport, and play. Therefore, they are sorry and angry (Rev. 12:12, 13). The devils see His hand at work and they are so upset that they are even preparing their own destruction while thinking that they are preparing for the destruction of others. The devils have been and still are leading the people away from the true God and His true religion, Islam.[285]

**Revelation 13:2 KJV-** And the beast which I saw was like unto a leopard, and his feet were as the feet of a bear, and his mouth as the mouth of a lion: and the dragon gave him his power, and his seat, and great authority.

**Revelation 13:2 NIV-** The beast I saw resembled a leopard, but had feet like those of a bear and a mouth like that of a lion. The dragon gave the beast his power and his throne and great authority.

> **HEM-** The Beast, Bible, Rev. 13:2 is the symbolic name of the ruler of the United States of America. It is a very bad and ugly name, but it is the truth, and very understandable, as we see it today. The dragon gives the beast power. Here recently, we have two presidents of the United States of America who have left the seat of authority and have flown to the Vatican

---

[285] Muhammad, *The Fall of America*, 72-73.

City of Rome to have an audience with the Pope of Rome in the hour of most needed advice. The Pope of Rome is the god of Christianity and not Jesus. The Pope rules the Christian world as a father rules his family. He is represented by some of the theologians in Christianity as being the Vice-General of God. But the prophets see him as far from being the Vice-General of God; otherwise they would not have given him the name, "dragon."[286]

**Revelation 13:4 KJV-** And they worshipped the dragon which gave power unto the beast: and they worshipped the beast, saying, Who is like unto the beast? Who is able to make war with him?

**Revelation 13:4 NIV-** Men worshiped the dragon because he had given authority to the beast, and they also worshiped the beast and asked, "Who is like the beast? Who can make war against him?

> **HEM-** Who is like unto the beast? Who is able to make war with him? (Rev. 13:4). This beast that is spoken of in the prophecy of the first book of the Bible called Revelations and has and still is being much misunderstood by my people. But one thing is certain, the name (beast) is believed by most all readers of the Book to refer to a person or persons, which is right. But who is the person or persons? (Note: There is mentioned in the same chapter and verse a dragon which gave power to the beast. Who can this dragon be? Is he also a person? Then how are the two related?)[287]

---

[286] Muhammad, *Our Saviour Has Arrived*, 204.
[287] Muhammad, *Message to the Blackman*, 124.

**Revelation 13:18 KJV-** Here is wisdom. Let him that hath understanding count the number of the beast: for it is the number of a man; and his number is Six hundred threescore and six.

**Revelation 13:18 NIV-** This calls for wisdom. If anyone has insight, let him calculate the number of the beast, for it is man's number. His number is 666.

> **HEM-** The eighteenth verse of the same chapter reads: Here is wisdom. Let him that hath understanding count the number of the beast: for it is the number of a man. Here we are told that the number of the beast referred to here is a man or people. Now the only way of knowing just what man or people is to watch and see what man or people's doings or works compare with the doings and works of the symbolic beast of the Revelation. This name beast, when given to a person, refers to that person's characteristics, not to an actual beast. Study the history of how America treats the freedom, justice and equality which is supposed to be given to all citizens of America (of course, the Negroes are not citizens of America). A citizen cannot and will not allow his people and government to treat him in such way as America treats her so-called Negroes.[288]

**Revelation 14:1 KJV-** And I looked, and, lo, a Lamb stood on the mount Sion, and with him an hundred forty and four thousand, having his Father's name written in their foreheads.

---

[288] Muhammad, *Message to the Blackman*, 124-25.

**Revelation 14:1 NIV-** Then I looked, and there before me was the Lamb, standing on Mount Zion, and with him 144,000 who had his name and his Father's name written on their foreheads.

> **HEM-** It is written (Rev. 14:1) that 144,000 of us will accept and return to our God and people and the rest of my people will go down with the enemies of Allah. For this sad prophecy of the loss of my people I write what I am writing, hoping perhaps that you may be able to beat the old prophets' predictions by making the truth so simple that a fool can understand it.[289]
>
> **HEM-** In the Bible, Rev. 14:1, we find the Lamb (Messenger of Allah, God) standing on the Mount Zion (foreign shore); with him was a hundred and forty four thousand (his followers who had escaped from the anger of the beast). The average so- called Negro preacher has always believed this was referring to Jesus, the son of Mary. But this is due to his lack of knowledge of the Bible story of Jesus. Jesus, as I have said and written, was only a prophet. He is not what the average so-called Negro is made to believe from the surface teachings of the Bible. They have been taught that Jesus is some kind of mysterious being, and not a natural man, and that he is God, and that he could be killed, put into a grave back there 2,000 years ago, and ascend up into space to await the end of the world. They have been taught to believe that he will return and usher in the Judgment of this world. All of this is wrong.[290]

---

[289] Muhammad, *Message to the Blackman*, 46.
[290] Muhammad, *Our Saviour Has Arrived*, 162-63.

**Revelation 14:4 KJV-** These are they which were not defiled with women; for they are virgins. These are they which follow the Lamb whithersoever he goeth. These were redeemed from among men, being the first fruits unto God and to the Lamb.

**Revelation 14:4 NIV-** These are those who did not defile themselves with women, for they kept themselves pure. They follow the Lamb wherever he goes. They were purchased from among men and offered as first fruits to God and the Lamb.

> **HEM-** The Bible's last book, under the title of Revelation of John, prophesies a grief falling upon the followers (the so-called American Negro) of the symbolic beast (the white man) who are in the beast's names and who worship and believe in the white man's religion, called Christianity. They worship the white man as though he were god above the Supreme God of heaven and earth. They also worship the white man's leader of the Christian religion, the Pope in Rome. This is mentioned in Revelation 14:4.[291]

**Revelation 14:15 KJV-** And another angel came out of the temple, crying with a loud voice to him that sat on the cloud, Thrust in thy sickle, and reap: for the time is come for thee to reap; for the harvest of the earth is ripe.

**Revelation 14:15 NIV-** Then another angel came out of the temple and called in a loud voice to him who was sitting

---

[291] Muhammad, *Message to the Blackman*, 263.

on the cloud, "Take your sickle and reap, because the time to reap has come, for the harvest of the earth is ripe."

> **HEM-** I think I have made it clear to you that if we look forward to seeing or meeting God, He must be in the form of a man. The Christians' Bible bears me witness that God is a man of flesh and blood. The Bible predicts God coming as a man (Luke 21:27; Matthew 24:30; Revelation 1:7, 14:15). There is much proof in the Bible to support my claim that God is man. That is, if you want proof. You have been taught so long that God is not a man, so you have become hardened against believing in anything other than what you have been taught.[292]

**Revelation 16:6 KJV-** For they have shed the blood of saints and prophets, and thou hast given them blood to drink; for they are worthy.

**Revelation 16:6 NIV-** For they have shed the blood of your saints and prophets, and you have given them blood to drink as they deserve.

> **HEM-** The slave-masters' every cry is to beat-beat-kill-kill-the so-called Negroes. Maybe the day has arrived that Allah will return to the devils- that which they have been so anxious to pour on the poor innocent so-called Negroes. Allah will give you your own blood to drink like water and your arms and allies will not help you against him. [293]

---

[292] Muhammad, *Our Saviour Has Arrived*, 72.
[293] Muhammad, *Message to the Blackman*, 128.

**Revelation 16:19 KJV-** And the great city was divided into three parts, and the cities of the nations fell: and great Babylon came in remembrance before God, to give unto her the cup of the wine of the fierceness of his wrath.

**Revelation 16:19 NIV-** The great city split into three parts, and the cities of the nations collapsed. God remembered Babylon the Great and gave her the cup filled with the wine of the fury of his wrath.

> **HEM-** The Revelations of John's prophecies were that they repented not of their evil deeds but blasphemed the very name of God (Rev. 16:9). Therefore, when a man is guilty of a great evil done against the cause of God and His people, he cannot be forgiven unless he seeks forgiveness himself. We see this in the working of the fall of America today. I say fall, for most surely this is the divine fall of America, as it was of ancient Babylon for its evils done to the Jews.[294]

> **HEM-** The die is set, with a foolish people, who like, in the time of Noah, could not see the sign of the rain, bringing on the Flood even after the clouds began to darken the sky. They did not see the on-coming rain until it actually started to rain. So it is with America. They pay no attention to the signs of the judgment that is now taking place. As the Bible prophesied in Rev. 16:9, they..."blasphemed the name of God, which hath power over these plagues...". How many in America and the city of Chicago disbelieve and even mock and swear at the Name of Allah, Who has power over the forces of nature on land, sea, and air.[295]

---

[294] Muhammad, *The Fall of America*, 132.
[295] Muhammad, *The Fall of America*, 213.

**Revelation 17:5 KJV-** And upon her forehead was a name written, MYSTERY, BABYLON THE GREAT, THE MOTHER OF HARLOTS AND ABOMINATIONS OF THE EARTH.

**Revelation 17:5 NIV-** This title was written on her forehead: MYSTERY BABYLON THE GREAT THE MOTHER OF PROSTITUTES AND OF THE ABOMINATIONS OF THE EARTH.

> **HEM-** In ancient times Babylon, under the Kings Nebuchadnezzar and Belshazzar, was the great city of idol worship and evil. She was the Queen of Evil -- rich and well fortified. But this "Mystery Babylon" must refer to a future city or people. No city or people answers the description better than the cities and people of America. This "Mystery Babylon" just could not be the ancient Babylon as we know her history.[296]
>
> **HEM-** The "Mystery Babylon, the Great" is none other than America. This "Mystery Babylon" is full of riches, hatred, filth, fornication, adultery, drunkenness, murder of the innocent and idol worship. "Mystery Babylon" is full of names of blasphemy. America is full of various religious faiths of the most ignorant kind. She was once the greatest slave buyer and seller. She has the greatest merchant marine service, the world's greatest export shippers in the merchandise of wheat, beasts, sheep, horses, chariots, gold, silver, iron, brass, wood, slaves, fine flour, corn and many others. You must know that all of the Revelation, or at least 90 percent, is directed to America. The seventeenth and

---

[296] Muhammad, *The Fall of America*, 129.

eighteenth chapters should open the so-called Negroes' eyes to the white race and white Christianity. There is no hereafter for the white race. Some few who are in Asia will stick around for a while.[297]

**Revelation 17:16 KJV-** And the ten horns which thou sawest upon the beast, these shall hate the whore, and shall make her desolate and naked, and shall eat her flesh, and burn her with fire.

**Revelation 17:16 NIV-** The beast and the ten horns you saw will hate the prostitute. They will bring her to ruin and leave her naked; they will eat her flesh and burn her with fire.

> **HEM-** I quote from Rev. 17:16, "And the ten horns which thou sawest upon the beast, these shall hate the whore...and shall eat her flesh, and burn her with fire!" The 'horns' here are a symbolic reference to Central and South America (America's satellites). This means that America's gifts and what-not will be accepted, but this does not mean that America has bought their sincere friendship. They will take all the gifts which America offers, but still this does not mean that America has their heart. America is careful not to give any help to her Black once-slave for four hundred years to do something for themselves. America wants to keep her Black slave tied while she watches their movements.[298]

## Revelation 18

---

[297] Muhammad, *The Fall of America*, 130.
[298] Ibid., 109.

> **HEM-** As the Prophet says in the 18th chapter; "She is a cage of every unclean and hateful bird." There are types of hateful birds. This is why a symbolical name is given. It means human beings. There are birds of prey and birds that are unclean such as crows, owls, buzzards and ravens that live and thrive off the carcass of others. And there are unclean people living and thriving off the unclean.[299]

**Revelation 18:2 KJV-** And he cried mightily with a strong voice, saying, Babylon the great is fallen, is fallen, and is become the habitation of devils, and the hold of every foul spirit, and a cage of every unclean and hateful bird.

**Revelation 18:2 NIV-** With a mighty voice he shouted: "Fallen! Fallen is Babylon the Great! She has become a home for demons and a haunt for every evil spirit, a haunt for every unclean and detestable bird.

> **HEM-** We can easily and truthfully liken the fall of America to the prophetic symbolic picture given in the (Bible) Revelation of John (18:2). The name Babylon used there does not really say whether it is ancient Babylon or a picture of some future Babylon. The description it gives is as follows: "And he [angel] cried mightily with a strong voice [with authority] saying, Babylon the great is fallen, is fallen and is become the habitation of devils [Allah has declared the people to be a race of devils], and the hole of every foul spirit and a cage of every unclean and hateful bird." The description here given to the Babylon by the Prophets

---

[299] Muhammad, *The Fall of America*, 90.

compares with the present history and people of America and their fall.[300]

**HEM-** The Bible refers to America by the name, Babylon, and teaches us, Rev. 18:2, "...Babylon the great is fallen, is fallen, and is become the habitation of devils, and the hole of every foul spirit, and a cage of every unclean and hateful bird." This is true, for America has accepted immigrants of the most evil and lewd character from Europe. America has filled her country with evil and indecency and there is no good in the works of America. America hates the doers of good and seeks to destroy them. This is the cause of the fall of America. You can bear witness to the deadly storms and twisters that are striking America in the areas where some of you live. Can you not see that Allah (God) is after you for the evil done to His people (Black man).[301]

**HEM-** The Revelation reads, in a prophecy relating to America, that she had in her a "hole for every foul spirit, and a cage of every unclean and hateful bird" (Revelation 18:2.) All hateful people have a haven to America. Though the scientists and scholars of the religion of Christianity know these words to be true, they desire yet to see the already-made blind, deaf and dumb so-called Negro go to his doom with them; and since they are by nature evil, they tempt them. The Holy Qur'an teaches that they only lead you to filth and evil. This is perfectly manifested today in America among its people ruled by the white man. The very

---

[300] Muhammad, *Message to the Blackman in America*, 276. See also, Muhammad, *The Fall of America*, 88.
[301] Muhammad, *The Fall of America*, 125.

conscience of an individual knows that these evils we see today are not accepted by God.[302]

**Revelation 18:4 KJV-** And I heard another voice from heaven, saying, Come out of her, my people, that ye be not partakers of her sins, and that ye receive not of her plagues.

**Revelation 18:4 NIV-** Then I heard another voice from heaven say: "Come out of her, my people, so that you will not share in her sins, so that you will not receive any of her plagues.

> **HEM-** Black Christian believers are warned in the Bible in the 18th Chapter of Revelation (last book) to come out of her ('her' means the way and belief of the white race and the so-called Christian religion) that we be not partakers with them in the Divine plagues of God upon her (U.S.A.). This is the religion that the prophets prophesied to you that the enemy will deceive you with. Christianity is not the teachings of Jesus. Their theologians and religious scientists will agree with us in a show-down that it was not the religion of Jesus; for the religion of Jesus was Islam as it was the religion of Moses and all the prophets of God. The Holy Qur'an teaches us that the prophets' religion was none other than Islam the religion of Truth, Freedom, Justice and Equality.[303]
>
> **HEM-** The so-called Negroes are warned to come out of her (America) (Rev. 18:4), though the truth of Daniel

---

[302] Muhammad, *The Fall of America*, 136.
[303] Muhammad, *Our Saviour Has Arrived*, 2-3.

and Revelations could not be told until the time of the end of this prophecy.[304]

**HEM-** America is falling. Her doom has come, and none said the prophets shall help her in the day of her downfall. In the Bible, God pleads with you to fly out of her (America) and seek refuge in Him (Rev. 18:4). What is going to happen in 1965 and 1966? It certainly will change your minds about following a doomed people, a people who hate you and your kind and who call one who teaches the truth about them a hater. They are the producers of hatred of us. We are with God and the righteous.[305]

**HEM-** The so-called American Negroes are referred to herein the 4th verse as being God's people ("My people") Come out of her...that ye be not partakers of her sins and that ye receive not of her plagues." This is a call to the American so-called Negroes to give up a doomed, wicked people that has destroyed them from being a people worthy of recognition, and who have now become lovers of their enemies and destroyers.[306]

**HEM-** Therefore, the Black man is warned in Rev. 18:4, "...Come out of her, my people..." This scripture warns the Black man to give up Babylon, which is a symbolic name, meaning America. America has tormented the Black Man. Now a tormentor is after her. The Divine Tormentor says, that we should not be partakers of the divine torment coming against America from Allah (God) Who came in the Person of Master Fard Muhammad, to Whom praises are due forever. This

---

[304] Muhammad, *Message to the Blackman*, 88.
[305] Ibid., 272-73.
[306] Muhammad, *The Fall of America*, 90.

means, "Separation." We must separate ourselves from America so that we will be saved from the stroke of the Master Who Is God Himself. Allah (God) is whipping America with all kinds of calamities.[307]

**HEM-** The last book of the Bible, the Revelations of John (18:4) makes this a little clearer. Both prophecies are similar but the one in Revelations is warning a people to flee out of Babylon so that they..."Be not partakers of her sins," of Babylon and receive not of her plagues."[308]

**Revelation 18:5 KJV-** For her sins have reached unto heaven, and God hath remembered her iniquities.

**Revelation 18:5 NIV-** For her sins are piled up to heaven, and God has remembered her crimes.

**HEM-** The 5th verse tells us that "Her sins have reached into heaven and God has remembered her iniquities and is ready to destroy her." Her destruction cometh quickly, according to the 8th verse, that plagues of death, mourning and famines which cometh in one day (one year) then after that she shall be destroyed by fire, utterly burned. This is backed up by the words: "Strong is the Lord God who judge her." Here it gives us a knowledge that He who judges is well able with power, with wisdom, and with deliberate and careful maneuvering to make judgment against her.[309]

---

[307] Muhammad, *The Fall of America*, 108.
[308] Ibid., 133-34.
[309] Ibid.

**HEM-** In the Bible, Rev. 18:4,5 in the Revelation of John, a people are warned to flee out of her. Here, we get the name Babylon to become a modern day people. The voice of an angel warns the people of a certain class to fly out of Babylon. "...Come out of her, my people, that ye be not partakers of her sins, and that ye receive not of her plagues. For her sins have reached unto heaven, and God hath remembered her iniquities" (as being an evil people). So the angel notifies us saying, "Babylon the great is fallen." Today, we see this same thing.[310]

**Revelation 18:6 KJV-** Reward her even as she rewarded you, and double unto her double according to her works: in the cup which she hath filled fill to her double.
**Revelation 18:6 NIV-** Give back to her as she has given; pay her back double for what she has done. Mix her a double portion from her own cup.

**HEM-** Here, the so-called Negro is warned to fly out of her and not to be partakers of her judgment -- her torment. The angel says, so much evil has she done to thee Rev. 18:6, "Reward her even as she rewarded you, and double unto her double according to her works: in the cup which she hath filled fill to her double." Allah (God) in the Person of Master Fard Muhammad, to Whom praises are due forever, said to me that there is nothing that you can do to her in the way of evil that could match the evil that she has already done to us.[311]

**Revelation 18:19 KJV-** And they cast dust on their heads, and cried, weeping and wailing, saying, Alas, alas that

---

[310] Muhammad, *The Fall of America*, 142.
[311] Ibid.

great city, wherein were made rich all that had ships in the sea by reason of her costliness! for in one hour is she made desolate.

**Revelation 18:19 NIV-** They will throw dust on their heads, and with weeping and mourning cry out: "Woe! Woe, O great city, where all who had ships on the sea became rich through her wealth! In one hour she has been brought to ruin!"

> **HEM-** This is America, the glory of the world in wealth, sport and play, with her merchant's ships ploughing the high seas carrying her costly merchandise throughout the population of the nations of the earth. (Bible, Rev. 18:19) The ships of America can be seen everywhere...in every port of the nations of earth. Her great navy is built to command the high seas. Her decks are mounted with great bristling rifle-barreled guns. The decks of her ships are covered with planes with which to carry deadly bomb-shells to pour on other nations who dare now to reject her entrance into their waters. The writer, (John), foresaw America threatening and daring the nations to disobey her order to allow her entrance. America's navy planes fly high in the air with their deadly bombs held ready to drop on the towns and cities of other nations who dare to attack her.[312]

**Revelation 19:20 KJV-** And the beast was taken, and with him the false prophet that wrought miracles before him, with which he deceived them that had received the mark of the beast, and them that worshipped his image. These

---

[312] Muhammad, *The Fall of America*, 124.

both were cast alive into a lake of fire burning with brimstone.

**Revelation 19:20 NIV-** But the beast was captured, and with him the false prophet who had performed the miraculous signs on his behalf. With these signs he had deluded those who had received the mark of the beast and worshiped his image. The two of them were thrown alive into the fiery lake of burning sulfur.

> **HEM-** The so-called Negroes are made so poisoned by this wicked race of devils that they love them more than they love their own people. It is really because of the evil done to them by the American white race that Allah (God) has put them on His list, as the first to be destroyed. The others will be given a little longer to live, as the prophet Daniel says (7:11 and Rev. 19:20).[313]

> **HEM-** Black Preachers, you will waste your time in leading yourself and those who follow you to hell by holding onto Christianity. Rev. 19:20. You cannot keep them in Christianity. Christianity was not the religion of Jesus, Moses or any of the prophets who came before them. It would have been a farce on the part of Allah (God) to have waited until just 2,000 years ago to give the right religion to the world of man. Allah (God) gave man the right religion, Islam, in the beginning of His creation of the heavens and the Earth. Allah (God) has not changed. His religion is Islam, entire Submission to His Will.[314]

---

[313] Muhammad, *Message to the Blackman in America*, 88.
[314] Muhammad, *The Fall of America*, 215.

**Revelation 20: 3-8 KJV-** And cast him into the bottomless pit, and shut him up, and set a seal upon him, that he should deceive the nations no more, till the thousand years should be fulfilled: and after that he must be loosed a little season. And I saw thrones, and they sat upon them, and judgment was given unto them: and I saw the souls of them that were beheaded for the witness of Jesus, and for the word of God, and which had not worshipped the beast, neither his image, neither had received his mark upon their foreheads, or in their hands; and they lived and reigned with Christ a thousand years. But the rest of the dead lived not again until the thousand years were finished.

This is the first resurrection. Blessed and holy is he that hath part in the first resurrection: on such the second death hath no power, but they shall be priests of God and of Christ, and shall reign with him a thousand years. And when the thousand years are expired, Satan shall be loosed out of his prison, And shall go out to deceive the nations which are in the four quarters of the earth, Gog, and Magog, to gather them together to battle: the number of whom is as the sand of the sea.

**Revelation 20: 3-8 NIV-** He threw him into the Abyss, and locked and sealed it over him, to keep him from deceiving the nations anymore until the thousand years were ended. After that, he must be set free for a short time. I saw thrones on which were seated those who had been given authority to judge. And I saw the souls of those who had been beheaded because of their testimony for Jesus and because of the word of God. They had not worshiped the beast or his image and had not received his mark on their foreheads or their hands. They came to life and reigned with Christ a thousand years. (The rest of the dead did not come to life until the thousand years were ended.)

This is the first resurrection. Blessed and holy are those who have part in the first resurrection. The second death has no power over them, but they will be priests of God and of Christ and will reign with him for a thousand years. When the thousand years are over, Satan will be released from his prison and will go out to deceive the nations in the four corners of the earth Gog and Magog to gather them for battle. In number they are like the sand on the seashore.

> **HEM-** More than anyone else, those who worship his image (the so-called Negroes) are guilty of loving the white race and all that race stands for. One can even find the pictures of white people on the walls, mantel, shelves, dressers and tables of their homes. Some carry them on their person. The so-called Negroes go to church and bow down to their statues under the name of Jesus and Mary and some under the name of Jesus' disciples, which are only the images of the white race, their arch-deceiver. They even worship the white race's names, which will not exist among the people of the new world, for they are not the names of God. [315]
> So a knowledge of the true God of Righteousness was not represented by the devils. The true God was not to be made manifest to the people until the god of evil (devil) has finished or lived out his time, which is

---

[315] Muhammad, *Message to the Blackman in America*, 83.

allowed to deceive the nations (read Thess. 2:9-10, Rev. 20:308-10).[316]

**HEM-** The shutting up and loosing of the devil mentioned in Rev. 20:7 could refer to the time between the A.D. 570-1555 when they (John Hawkins) deceived our fathers and brought them into slavery in America, which is nearly 1,000 years that they and Christianity were bottled up in Europe by the spread of Islam by Muhammad (may the peace of Allah be upon him) and his successors.[317]

**HEM-** As you have in the Bible, Lucifer's (Yakub) fall also represents the fall of his race. The lake or sea in which they choked and perished in is the same lake mentioned in the Revelations of John- that all that had the mark of the beast, the representatives of the beast and the false prophets (priests and preachers of Christianity) referred to as being cast alive in a lake of fire.[318]

**Revelation 20:10-14 KJV-** And the devil that deceived them was cast into the lake of fire and brimstone, where the beast and the false prophet are, and shall be tormented day and night for ever and ever. And I saw a great white throne, and him that sat on it, from whose face the earth and the heaven fled away; and there was found no place for them. And I saw the dead, small and great, stand before God; and the books were opened: and another book was opened, which is the book of life: and the dead were judged out of those things which were written in the

---

[316] Muhammad, *Message to the Blackman*, 2.
[317] Ibid., 3
[318] Muhammad, *How to Eat to Live I*, 74.

books, according to their works. And the sea gave up the dead which were in it; and death and hell delivered up the dead which were in them: and they were judged every man according to their works. And death and hell were cast into the lake of fire. This is the second death.

**Revelation 20:10-14 NIV-** And the devil, who deceived them, was thrown into the lake of burning sulfur, where the beast and the false prophet had been thrown. They will be tormented day and night forever and ever. Then I saw a great white throne and him who was seated on it. Earth and sky fled from his presence, and there was no place for them. And I saw the dead, great and small, standing before the throne, and books were opened. Another book was opened, which is the book of life. The dead were judged according to what they had done as recorded in the books. The sea gave up the dead that were in it, and death and Hades gave up the dead that were in them, and each person was judged according to what he had done. Then death and Hades were thrown into the lake of fire. The lake of fire is the second death.

> **HEM-** We want separation. We want a home on this earth we can call our own. We want to go for self and leave the enemy who has been sentenced to death by Allah (Rev. 20:10-14) from the day he was created (See this subject in the Bible and Qur-an). No one, white, black, brown, yellow or red can prove to me by any scriptures of Allah (God) sent by one of the prophets of Allah (God) that we should not be separated from the white race, that we should believe and follow the religion dictated, shaped and formed by the theologians of the white race. The coming Allah and

the judgment of the wicked world is made clear by the prophetic sayings of the Prophets. The so-called reverends and the proud intellectual class are doomed to destruction with the enemy, if they remain with him instead of joining onto Allah, Who loves them and Who will deliver them and the Nation of Islam.[319]

**Revelation 20:15 KJV-** And whosoever was not found written in the book of life was cast into the lake of fire.

**Revelation 20:15 NIV-** If anyone's name was not found written in the book of life, he was thrown into the lake of fire.

> **HEM-** Read your Bible; it is there in the last Book. Revelations warns you that all who have the name of the beast are pushed into hell fire - all of the beast's disciples or false prophets such as the preachers of the Christian religion and those who are helping the beast to deceive us, as they are deceived. Read your Bible. It teaches us that they were blind teachers who could not lead a seeing one, nor could they lead another blind one; for they are blind themselves.[320]

**Revelation 21:1 KJV-** And I saw a new heaven and a new earth: for the first heaven and the first earth were passed away; and there was no more sea.

**Revelation 21:1 NIV-** Then I saw a new heaven and a new earth, for the first heaven and the first earth had passed away, and there was no longer any sea.

---

[319] Muhammad, *Message to the Blackman,* 72.
[320] Muhammad, *Our Saviour Has Arrived,* 79. See the same words of the Honorable Elijah Muhammad sited, Muhammad, **Fall of America**, 178.

**HEM-** Go to Asia or Africa and you will hear more about the happiness of the people over what Allah has revealed to me than among the American Black people. They all know that it is the truth that they have been waiting to learn for 6,000 years. Read Isaiah 65:17 and 66:22 and Revelation 21:1 of the Bible. Read the second Surah of the Holy Qur'an. The new generation will be raised up. My main mission and work, put upon me by Allah (God), in the Person of Master Fard Muhammad, to Whom Praise is due forever, is to put you on the right path so you may go for self under the guidance of Almighty God Allah in the Person of Master Fard Muhammad. He (meaning Master Fard Muhammad) will end the present conflict between the slave and his master. If they will do anything for us of good, they will be rewarded for that good act by Allah (God), Master Fard Muhammad, and they know this.[321]

**Revelation 21:5 KJV-** And he that sat upon the throne said, Behold, I make all things new. And he said unto me, Write: for these words are true and faithful.

**Revelation 21:5 NIV-** He who was seated on the throne said, "I am making everything new!" Then he said, "Write this down, for these words are trustworthy and true.

> **HEM-** Rev: 21:5 What Will Become of the old? We must have a new government, a new ruler and a teacher of that new government, since it is not patterned after the order of the old government (world). As the God of Truth, Justice, and Righteousness, Allah Is Going to Be the Ruler or the Creator of the New Government. Then by no means

---

[321] Muhammad, *Our Saviour Has Arrived*, 112-13.

can He Carry any of the old world into His New Kingdom of Truth, Justice, Equality, and Peace.[322]

**HEM-** The new world of Islam is coming in - not the old world of Islam, but a new world of Islam. 'Behold I make all things new!' Rev. 21:5. We are living in the change of worlds. The old world is going out and the new world is coming in. This is something to be happy and thankful to Allah for- to bear witness to the change of worlds![323]

**HEM-** It is necessary for me to consult or refer to the Bible for this subject. It can be found in the Holy Qur-an, but not in the exact words as are found in the Bible. So, because of the truth of it, and because my people do not know any Scripture or ever read any Scripture other than the Bible (which they do not understand), I thought it best to make them understand the book which they read and believe in, since the Bible is their graveyard and they must be awakened from it. There are many Muslims who do not care to read anything in the Bible. But those Muslims have not been given my job. Therefore, I ignore what they say and write! By all means, we must get the "truth" to our people (the so-called Negroes), for the time is limited. The coming of a "New World" or a new order of things is very hard for the people of the Old World to believe. Therefore, they are opposed to the New World.[324]

**Revelation 21:8 KJV-** But the fearful, and unbelieving, and the abominable, and murderers, and whoremongers, and sorcerers, and idolaters, and all liars, shall have their part

---

[322] Muhammad, *Our Saviour Has Arrived*, 113.
[323] Ibid., 144
[324] Muhammad, *Message to the Blackman*, 82-83.

in the lake which burneth with fire and brimstone: which is the second death.

**Revelation 21:8 NIV-** But the cowardly, the unbelieving, the vile, the murderers, the sexually immoral, those who practice magic arts, the idolaters and all liars—their place will be in the fiery lake of burning sulfur. This is the second death.

> **HEM-** There are so many places that I could point out in the Bible and Holy Qur'an that warn us of fearing our enemies above or equal to the fear of Allah (God). It is a fool who has a greater fear of the devils (white man) than Allah who has the power to destroy the devils and their followers (Rev. 21:8; Holy Qur'an 7:18 and 15:43). We must remember that if Islam means entire submission to the will of Allah, that and that alone is the True religion of Allah. Do not you and your religious teachers and the Prophets of old teach that the only way to receive God's help or Guidance is to submit to his will! -then WHY NOT ISLAM! It ( Islam) is the true religion of Allah and the ONLY way to success.[325]

> **HEM-** It is a shame to see our people in such fearful condition. "The fearful and the unbelieving shall have their part in the lake which burns with fire and brimstone which is the second death". (Rev. 21:8) The devil whom they fear more than Allah (God) was not able to protect himself against Allah; therefore his followers shared with him the fire of hell. They had suffered one death (mental), and by fearing the devils

---

[325] Muhammad, *Message to the Blackman*, 29-30.

and rejecting the truth, they suffered a physical death, which was the final death.[326]

---

[326] Muhammad, *Message to the Blackman*, 99.

# Coming Soon!

To order an advanced copy of *O' You Who Believe*, contact:

A-Team Publishing

PO Box 551036

Atlanta, GA 30355

ATeamPublishing.com